T

Coey/Cowie Brothers

All Railwaymen

by

John Chacksfield,

FBIS, AFAIAA, MRAeS, C.Eng

THE OAKWOOD PRESS

© Oakwood Press & John Chacksfield 2003

British Library Cataloguing in Publication Data
A Record for this book is available from the British Library
ISBN 0 85361 605 1

Typeset by Oakwood Graphics.
Repro by Ford Graphics, Ringwood, Hants.
Printed by Inkon Printers Ltd, Yateley, Hants.

A fine portrait of B&NCR 2-4-0 No. 52.

Title page: GS&WR Aspinall class '60' No. 95 pilots Coey class '321' No. 328 on a heavy express in the latter days of steam in Ireland. Both locomotives have been rebuilt and No. 95 still sports the original type of tender having 2,730 gallon capacity which first appeared on this batch. The front coach is a rarity in Ireland, a 12-wheeled clerestory brake composite, which is followed by a 1905 8-compartment corridor type, then a post-war Bredin coach with what appears to be another 8-compartment corridor in different livery. The date of this photograph is unknown, but the colour light signal visible over the fifth coach would appear to put it in the early 1950s. This makes the class '60' at least 75 years of age, with the class '321' a mere stripling at only 50! *CIE*

Front cover: Robert Coey GS&WR 4-4-0 No. 321 with the American Mail depicted on a period picture postcard. *John Alsop Collection*
Rear cover, top: B&NCR 4-4-0 compound No. 62. *Railway Magazine*
Rear cover, bottom: Turbine steamer *Princess Maud* at Larne. *John Alsop Collection*

Published by The Oakwood Press (Usk), P.O. Box 13, Usk, Mon., NP15 1YS.
E-mail: oakwood-press@dial.pipex.com
Website: www.oakwood-press.dial.pipex.com

Contents

A 1905 photograph of the Coey/Parkhill families. *Back row, left to right:* Ernest Parkhill (son of James and Catherine (née Coey) Parkhill), Ivy Parkhill (daughter of Robert and Mary (née Coey) Parkhill), Revd James W. Parkhill, Robert (Bobby) Parkhill (son of Robert and Mary), Edith Parkhill (daughter of Robert and Mary), Harold Parkhill (son of James and Catherine), *Front row, left to right:* Lillian Parkhill (daughter of Robert and Mary), Walter Parkhill (son of James and Catherine), Sarah Coey, James Coey, Mary Parkhill, Robert Parkhill, Catherine Parkhill, Robert A. Parkhill (on Catherine's lap) father of Anne Parkhill.

Anne Parkhill

Foreword

I feel very honoured to have been invited to write the foreword to this book on my great uncles Robert, James and Henry, the Coey/Cowie brothers. I did not have the privilege of knowing them personally because of the generation gap, but from my childhood I heard from time to time about my 'great uncles in the railways'. It was not until years later through conversations with my cousins in England and Ireland, who as children had met James and Henry, and conversations with Robert's daughter Maud shortly before she died, that I began to grasp their importance in the railway world as men of considerable repute in Ireland - Robert the engineer and James and Henry the administrators.

John Chacksfield has written an absorbing account of the three brothers, skilfully interweaving their careers with the joys and sorrows of their families, spanning the period from the 1880s to the 1930s, set against the backcloth of the economic, political and social changes and events taking place in Ireland and on the wider stage at the time. Not least was the momentous event of the launching of the ill-fated *Titanic* in Belfast in 1911. The result is an illuminating insight into the history of two of the most important railway networks in Ireland during this period - the Great Southern & Western Railway (GS&WR) and the Belfast & Northern Counties Railway (B&NCR), viewed through the careers and experiences of these three remarkable men - Robert as Works Manager and then Locomotive Superintendent of the GS&WR at Inchicore, Dublin, James as Secretary and General Manager of the B&NCR at York Street Terminus, Belfast and Henry as chief clerk of the B&NCR (Northern Counties Committee).

Robert and James were pioneers in their own right, creating and presiding over innovative and far-reaching changes in the evolving railway scene. As the book reveals, their careers touched those of other well-known railwaymen including McDonnell, Aspinall, Ivatt and Maunsell, Locomotive Superintendents of the GS&WR, and Edward Cotton and Bowman Malcolm, General Manager and Locomotive Superintendent respectively of the B&NCR. The book analyses the achievements of the three brothers objectively, covering in detail the expansion of rail route mileage on both networks; locomotive, carriage and waggon developments; the expansion and consolidation of rail/boat links with the mainland; the development of railway linked tourism and rail/road linked transport services in the north of Ireland; and the main administrative changes which took place.

This book is a fitting tribute to these three brothers who left their mark on the railway scene in Ireland in the closing years of the 19th century and the early years of the 20th, when railways reigned supreme.

Anne Parkhill
Stafford

Preamble and Acknowledgements

Having bitten the bullet and covered R.E.L. Maunsell in a biography, certain information associated with his predecessor at Inchicore works of the Great Southern & Western Railway, Robert Coey, was collected. Examination of this suggested that here was a further engineer of note to eminate from Ireland, and who would be well worth writing about. Little has been published about Coey, and having considerable detail to draw upon from my data on Maunsell, I determined to see what could be put together from these earlier researches.

As time progressed, it was apparent that something of substance could be created, more particularly when I realised that Coey had two brothers, Henry and James Cowie, also choosing the railway as a career in Belfast. With the differing spelling of the surname in the Scottish based 'Cowie' and the Irish version 'Coey', it had not been immediately clear that the link between Belfast and Dublin was so close.

Archive material on Robert Coey and his brothers is very limited, but through a relative Anne Parkhill, a great-niece, I was able to gather much family data, including all the family photographs used in the illustration of this book. She also provided copies of Robert Coey's letters to his brother-in-law, the Revd James Parkhill (her grandfather) written from Switzerland and Italy during his extensive travels in retirement. In this connection I must acknowledge the contributions made by Rhona and Barry Leigh and Elizabeth Hunter in providing anecdotal information and photographs on James and Henry, and Archie Wood who researched Methodist Church records and the General Register Office in Belfast on the history of James' children. I must express my further grateful thanks to Anne Parkhill, firstly for her most generous Foreword and secondly for her patient reading of my draft text to ensure that the family information included is correct.

Correspondence between Coey's daughter, Maud, and the National Railway Museum, just before she died, produced some useful information on his retirement days and, also some helpful facts covering his time as Locomotive Superintendent. The Irish Railways, CIE at Inchicore, through their Chief Mechanical Engineer, John McCarthy, once again very kindly dug into their archives for me, as did the Engineering Department of Queen's University in Belfast. The Railway Collection of the Ulster Folk Museum also proffered some information, and I am indebted to my other contacts via George Carpenter at his luncheon club held each Thursday at the Institution of Civil Engineers. In particular I would like to express my thanks to Jim Jarvis, who provided many of the photographs of GS&WR and B&NCR (NCC) locomotives from his collection of glass slides. He also arranged for me to have access to his late brother Ron's collection which now resides at the Midland Railway Trust.

When it came to planning this book, I felt that to avoid any confusion of dates and events, the two disciplines, Engineering and Administration, which were chosen by the brothers, would be covered in separate sections, as their respective careers in those areas overlapped crucial times in the railway history of Ireland, both North and South. Therefore the first section covers the engineering exploits of Robert, which had a far-reaching and lasting impact on the many locomotive developments in the express, goods and general purpose fleets produced and maintained at Inchicore in the closing years of the 19th century and the first decade of the 20th. The second section deals with James and Henry and their lengthy administrative careers in Belfast at the headquarters of the Belfast & Northern Counties Railway. This subsequently became the Northern Counties Committee (NCC) of the Midland Railway which, at Grouping, was to become part of the London, Midland and Scottish Railway (LMS).

Introduction

It took Alexander McDonnell's organisational expertise to obtain order out of the chaotic situation of the locomotive stock of the Great Southern & Western Railway which he found upon his taking office in 1864 as Locomotive Superintendent. His ensuing legacy of standard designs was continued by Aspinall and Ivatt until the mid-1890s, with minimal changes, and the addition of only a small number of new designs in the form of tank engines and derivatives of his early 4-4-0s. As the 20th century approached, Robert Coey, succeeding Ivatt in 1896, developed a range of new express and goods locomotives, the former to cater for the increased train weights caused by the introduction of bogie stock, the latter to supplement the prolific, but dated, existing 0-6-0 fleet developed from a McDonnell introduction of 1867. In addition the route mileage of the GS&WR was rapidly expanding (from 565 miles of 1895 to 1,150 miles in 1901) as it absorbed smaller concerns. A fair proportion of the locomotive stock of these railways needed replacing by more modern types.

Coey's engineering expertise and willingness to introduce new technology as it became available, ensured that the motive power fleet was kept up-to-date and fully capable of carrying out its duties. Inchicore works was modernised and expanded to cope with most of the locomotive building programme over the 15 years of his incumbency, this largely due to the expertise of his deputy and Works Manager, Richard Maunsell. The net result was that the GS&WR obtained a stock of reliable and solid designs, many of which lasted until the final days of steam in Ireland.

The story of how this took place is contained in the first part of this book, the story of Robert Coey's life and career; a largely unsung career yet, on analysis, we find an extremely capable and practical engineer. His locomotive developments were well up with similar happenings on the mainland. So often we tend to dismiss the Irish railway scene as casual and outmoded, forgetting that many eminent railway engineers came from that land. Robert Coey was one such engineer.

In the Appendix the reader will find a performance analysis of one of Robert Coey's express 4-4-0s which is compared with further 4-4-0 developments in later years of R.E.L. Maunsell. This analysis indicates that Coey was equal to many other eminent engineers on the other side of the Irish Sea. Maunsell was for long an exponent of the 4-4-0 and it seems clear that the improvements he made to this classic layout were based on the solid experience he had gained whilst working with Coey at Inchicore, for his job as Works Manager often brought him into close liaison with the design office.

Robert had two brothers, James and Henry who, according to railway records, chose the Scottish spelling of the family name, Cowie, in connection with their profession, although there is evidence that the only one to do this permanently was James. This sometimes confusing choice is discussed fully in the opening Chapter. They both chose the administration sphere of the Belfast & Northern Counties Railway in Ulster as a career, so the experiences in the management area of these two are also covered to complete the picture of a rather unique family. It also provides an ideal medium for comparison between the Dublin (GS&WR) and Belfast (B&NCR) involvements in the railway scene in Ireland prior to partition, in addition to covering the initial years of the NCC after partition.

Opportunity has been taken in the second part of this story to briefly cover the locomotive and rolling stock developments during the years of James's and Henry's employment on the B&NCR (NCC) to give a comparison with the GS&WR types attributed to Robert Coey which are covered comprehensively in the first part.

Robert Coey.   *Anne Parkhill*

Chapter One

Robert Coey - Engineer:
The Early Years

Before launching into the stories of the brothers, there is one matter to try and put into order regarding the family surname: Robert Coey, James Cowie, Henry Cowie, Mary Coey, Catherine Coey and Elizabeth Coey were all brothers and sisters. Their father was James COEY, whose own father had, it is fairly certain, spelt the family name COWIE. Some confusion appears to be abroad with the family name. We know, from legal documents, that James, the father was definitely known as COEY in the times covered by this narrative, but it is not exactly clear why two of the children used COWIE.

The family roots are Scottish and COWIE is a recognised Scottish surname of which COEY is the Irish equivalent. It seems that one of the male members of the family born in Belfast, James, used the Scottish spelling which suited him for some reason despite the inevitable problems this might entail, even going so far as to have it ratified by Deed Poll. Henry, however, even though he appears as Cowie in the railway documentation, never completely adopted that spelling, as legal documents accredited to him are to be found under the Coey spelling. There is also a legend in the family that the spelling turned on the pronunciation, 'Coey' being preferred to 'Cow-ie' by the majority of the family.

For this book the spelling preferred (if that indeed was the case) by the individuals in connection with their careers will be used, as much of the documentation available for research has confirmed. Be that as it may, we have a unique family, in that all three brothers became railwaymen of some considerable repute at a time when the railway was an expanding prime mover throughout the world's developing countries. Their respective lives are inextricably bound up in engineering and management decisions which shaped the Irish railway developments over half a century of progress in that land.

Not too much has been written over recent years about the Irish railway scene and those engineers and managers responsible for its development. Some eminent authors have produced comprehensive accounts of motive power development and railways constructed in that land. All too often we tend to regard Ireland as a backwater of engineering technology, yet the English scene has benefited considerably by the injection of persons such as Richard Maunsell, who was, between the wars, one of the 'Big Four' CMEs, and we begin to understand the expertise which has grown from small railways in Ireland and their effects on locomotive development and management styles in particular.

The largest railway works in Ireland was built up at Inchicore, on the south-western fringes of Dublin. Constructed by the Great Southern & Western Railway in 1846, the works still exist, and constitute the largest engineering complex of its kind in the Republic of Ireland. The factory buildings are a gem of Victorian industrial architecture. Constructed of blue limestone, they are distinctively castellated in their design and were built at a total cost of £236,208, but contemporary accounts state that this considerable expenditure includes all

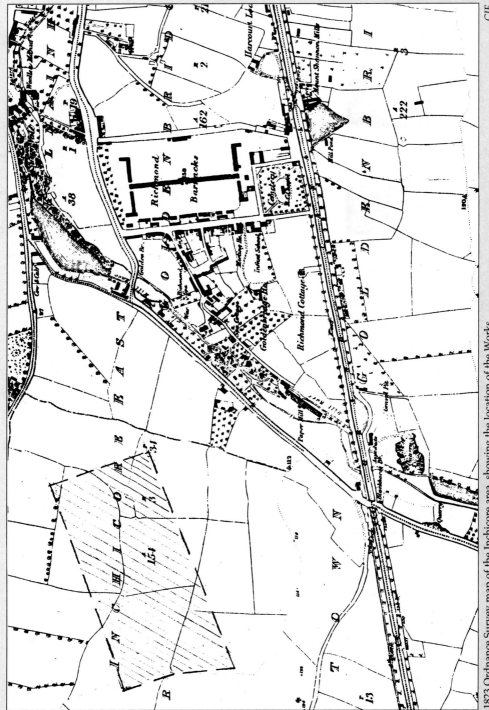

1823 Ordnance Survey map of the Inchicore area, showing the location of the Works.

The early locomotives on the GS&WR were Bury, Curtis and Kennedy 2-2-2s. One example, No. 36, has survived to this day, after no less than three preservation exercises! In Coey's day it was to be found on a plinth in the grassed area next to the office block. It is now to be seen on permanent exhibition in Kent station, Cork. Built 1847, withdrawn 1874 after running 360,000 miles.   *CIE*

the locomotive facilities at other parts of the line then existing, also the company houses provided for many of the workforce. The old Inchicore running shed, eventually amalgamated into the works when its larger modern replacement was built, was fronted by an imposing castellated facade. The architect for this building, which still stands today, was Sancton Wood. One particular feature of Wood's design, which also still exists today, is the tower placed on the side bordering the main line. This originally had a specific purpose, that of providing a perch for 'lookout' men who, before any meaningful signalling existed, kept a watch on train movements locally. Needless to say, this rather primitive system was replaced at an early stage by a semaphore system operated from a conventional signal cabin.

From the earliest days of Alexander McDonnell's installation as Locomotive Superintendent, Inchicore was gradually expanded to be a model of self-sufficiency. Everything that it was possible to make with adequate economy was made there, with the result that expensive imports from the mainland were kept to a minimum. The saw mills were kept busy producing raw sleepers for the creosote plant, and all the gas needed for the works and the Kingsbridge terminus came from the works on site. Many of the peripheral trappings of a railway, such as lamps, tables, luggage barrows, etc. were manufactured there. In 1877, Alexander McDonnell, in his drive to update Inchicore works fully, installed the first iron rolling mill in Ireland, the motive power to drive this coming from the conversion of an old withdrawn Bury engine. Very similar to the mill at Crewe, on which it had been based, it was under the control of a foreman specially trained at that plant. The iron to feed the mill was supplied from two Siemens furnaces, initially peat fired but eventually coal fired, once this latter imported fuel became cheaper than peat.

Through the years of the mid to late 19th century and the first years of the 20th century, Inchicore had some very eminent Locomotive Superintendents as well as McDonnell, namely, Aspinall, Ivatt, Coey and Maunsell. Although Aspinall and Ivatt were English, they gained at Inchicore much of their early experience in the day-to-day running of a complex railway works and the associated design expertise needed to produce new and improved locomotives and rolling stock. It was a good training ground. The other three were all Irish by birth, McDonnell and Maunsell from Dublin and Coey from Belfast.

Robert Coey, Locomotive Superintendent at Inchicore from 1896 to 1911, is an interesting character, and his career forms the core of the first part of this book. He was an extremely capable and experienced engineer, having a good theoretical grasp of matters pertaining to locomotive design. He also was a capable administrator and planner and, additionally, very cost-concious. Within the constraints in which he had to work, he managed well, with few failures or disappointments. Compared to some of his predecessors he achieved the top job at a mature 45 years of age and was able to apply his very considerable expertise to the matters needing his attention. He presided over the GS&WR locomotive, carriage and wagon requirements at a time when considerable expansion was taking place as other railways were being absorbed into the network. The pressure associated with this job, as we shall see, was high and sometimes relentless, and the demands on his judgement and expertise came thick and fast. If he had a fault, it was to limit the delegation of some tasks only to those in whom he had absolute trust and confidence, whilst keeping the rest for his own consideration. His attention to detail was, at all times, meticulous and probably these features led to his breakdown in health as the years progressed.

This section of the book describes Robert's life and career on the GS&WR at a time when many improvements in locomotive technology were emerging. As we shall see, such improvements did not pass him by.

Born in 1851 at the family home, 2 Letitia Street, Belfast (in the same year as John Aspinall and Henry Ivatt, with both of whom Robert was to pass an important phase in his engineering career), he was the eldest of four boys and three girls, the children of James and Sarah(née Brown) Coey, who had married on 5th September, 1850. From the age of about six or seven he was educated at the Belfast Model School, which in those days would not have provided much in the way of engineering or the sciences. However, some interest and encouragement in engineering would have come from his father, also an engineer by profession. When his schooldays came to an end in 1866, the Coey family, by this time living at 23 Wilson Street, was still growing, with the addition that year of William. However, William died at the age of 10 in 1876, and is buried in the family grave in Belfast City cemetery, the first family member to occupy the grave plot purchased by James Coey Snr in that year.

Upon leaving school, Robert was apprenticed to Victor Coates & Co. Ltd, engineers and boilermakers, at the Lagan Foundry, Belfast, which was engaged in designing and building steam engines for the local industry. His technical skills were honed during this apprenticeship, at the end of which, in 1871, he enrolled at the College of Science in Dublin to increase his theoretical

James (senior) and Sarah Coey   *Anne Parkhill*

knowledge. His enquiring mind wished to find out more about the technical matters associated with his chosen profession of engineering. Here his abilities won him a Whitworth Scholarship in Mechanical Science to Queen's College, Belfast. He duly returned to his home city to commence his studies in 1872, living at home, by now 17 Wilson Street. He was, by all accounts, a model student, with many awards for his efforts throughout his time at Queen's. His first year of the three year course resulted in prizes for studies in Experimental Physics, Engineering, Drawing and Office Work, in his second year for Mathematical Physics, Civil Engineering and Office Work, finishing off with final year prizes for Engineering, Natural Philosophy (Applied), Civil and Mechanical Engineering and Office Work. In 1875 he graduated with a Bachelor of Engineering degree with First Class Honours and immediately returned to Dublin where he obtained a position as draughtsman with the Dublin Port and Docks Board. The Chief Engineer of this concern was a Brindon B. Stoney, who quickly realised the ability of this bright young graduate from Belfast. He ensured that he was kept well-informed as to the progress of Robert in his relatively junior position.

Following some months in the drawing office of the Board, Coey was promoted to the position of Clerk of Works by Stoney, who had, by now, decided that he had a thoroughly competent and quick learning junior under him. In this position he was to oversee the rebuilding of the Carlisle Bridge and construction of the new iron swing (Butt) bridge. Never one to sit on the sidelines, Robert took an active interest in the underwater work associated with the substantial foundations required for these structures, going so far as to don

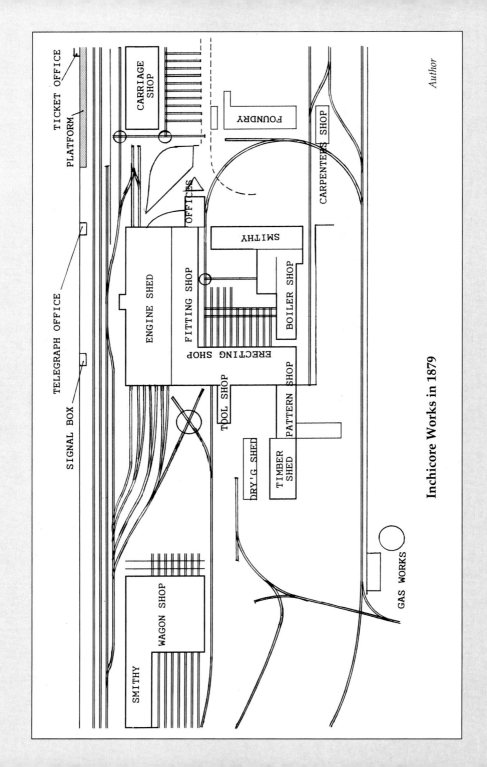

Inchicore Works in 1879

Author

a diving suit for some investigation in the dim, murky depths of the Liffey. He recounted a tale to Ernest Joynt, who became his chief draughtsman in later years, of losing his hold on the guiding rope on one of his dives and taking some 30 minutes groping in the waters before finding it and regaining the surface.

Although an extremely capable civil engineer, Coey found the pace somewhat slow and so in 1880, after nearly four years, resigned his Clerk of Works position and joined the drawing office staff at Inchicore as a draughtsman. Here his undoubted abilities were recognised and he soon found himself involved with the current development work on the locomotive stock. His technical expertise was noted by McDonnell, who recognised at an early stage the potential of this well-qualified young engineer as a high-flyer. In the words of Ernest Joynt, who was to be one of his close associates in his locomotive superintendency years: 'He was a man of great but quiet energy of character, possessed of a firm will, and using much judgement in his decisions. He was of a thoughtful habit, parsimonious of speech, but when he expressed himself, his words, if few, were clear and to the point'. Here we have the first statement as to his temperament, a studious and serious person who took his responsibilities very much to heart. His daughter Maud described him as being a very serious, rather dour, individual, although photographs of him in retirement show a relaxed and almost genial looking person. Never a very communicative sort, except where matters of extreme technical content of immediate interest were concerned, he could, at first sight, be thought to be aloof from the more personal problems associated with his associates. This was not the case, however, as he could certainly show understanding and sympathy where needed. His theoretical knowledge on engineering matters plus his practical expertise ensured that he was to be nurtured by his superiors for future advancement.

We now need to look at the next phase in Robert's career. The railways were still growing in importance as an effective transport medium and Inchicore works already was acknowledged as a leader in Ireland in its provision of locomotives and rolling stock for the GS&WR. Contemporary reports placed it equal to the larger concerns in Great Britain in terms of technical expertise and manufacturing quality. We shall see, over the next few Chapters, just how much Robert's time at Inchicore, during which he advanced to the top, helped to shape the engineering aspects of this major Irish railway as it expanded over the remaining years of the 19th century and into the initial years of the next one.

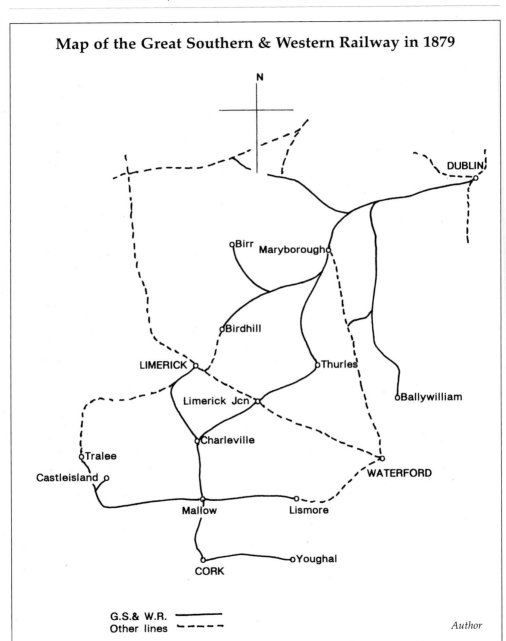

Map of the Great Southern & Western Railway in 1879

Chapter Two

The Move to Inchicore

In assessing the motive power situation on the GS&WR when Robert Coey joined the design staff in 1880, it may help to summarise the reorganisation and standardisation policies wrought under the leadership of Alexander McDonnell (1829-1904) between 1864 and 1882.

In 1864, McDonnell was appointed Locomotive Superintendent in place of George Miller who had died in January of that year. A Dublin doctor's son, he entered Trinity College in 1847 and graduated with a BA degree in 1852. He then departed for England to learn his engineering profession, eventually working under Charles Liddell on the construction of railways in the West of England until 1857, after which he became the Locomotive Superintendent of the Newport, Abergavenny & Hereford Railway, where he had charge over a fleet of 26 engines. After five years in that capacity he travelled to Eastern Europe to initiate the locomotive department of the Danube and Black Sea Railway, before the opportunity to return to Ireland occurred.

Upon his taking up the reins at Inchicore, he set about reorganising the stock of locomotives, then consisting of a multitude of types from a range of manufacturers: Bury, Rothwell, Sharp, and Fairbairn in addition to Inchicore designs of Wakefield and Miller. Little account as to standardisation of parts had been taken over the years, and with a fleet of 57 passenger engines of nine different classes plus 47 goods engines of a staggering 13 classes, matters were far from ideal. Hence his first task was to organise the workshop side of the plant in order to get the best out of a very mixed bag of largely obsolescent types. Having started to improve the availability, he turned his mind to preparing some standard designs. Initially three were planned, for express (2-4-0), passenger (2-4-0) and goods (0-6-0). These were followed later by two standard tank designs, for passenger (0-4-4T) and shunting (0-6-4T) work respectively. These latter types were the medium for the introduction of the American swing-link bogie to the Irish railway scene. The 0-4-4Ts were well tanks and had originally been built as single boiler Fairlies, but after a brief time in traffic were rebuilt as conventional tanks. Of the tender types, the 2-4-0s were to be developed into 4-4-0s after a few years, again using the swing-link bogie. McDonnell was eventually to take this new development to the North Eastern Railway, Aspinall to the Lancashire & Yorkshire and Ivatt to the Great Northern. He is also credited with the introduction of the cast metal number plate for locomotives, something normally attributed to Webb on the London & North Western Railway (LNWR), but McDonnell had introduced this feature before Webb became CME at Crewe.

This legacy of standard designs was used by both Aspinall and Ivatt for their offerings in the motive power sphere during their respective incumbencies as Locomotive Superintendent Aspinall from 1882 to 1886 and Ivatt from 1886 to 1896.

McDonnell was a gifted organiser and, throughout his tenure of the locomotive superintendency, Inchicore became established as an engineering

Alexander McDonnell.   *CIE*

concern equal to any on the mainland. We have already seen his expertise in the expansion of the works in the previous Chapter, and it will be appropriate to examine the effects of his hand on the locomotive stock. The costs associated with the building of engines were strictly controlled, by recycling materials from withdrawn types, and as the standard designs replaced the obsolescent engines, the stocks of spares became more easily manageable. In 1877, the first McDonnell 4-4-0 was produced, starting a legacy of 35 years' development of this classic layout at Inchicore. In fact when we look at the passenger locomotives built for the GS&WR over the 60 years from 1853 to 1912 we see that out of the 124 such types constructed, some 76, or 61 per cent, were 4-4-0s, most of the remainder being the closely related 2-4-0s.

The large building programme initiated by McDonnell resulted in the 100th new locomotive of this programme emerging from the works in 1879, and on 8th August the event was celebrated by a gala sports day, dinner and ball for the Inchicore workforce and their families. To all accounts it was a grand day, with even the dubious Irish weather smiling on the occasion, for the anticipated rain did not materialise.

In 1880, some two years prior to McDonnell's departure for the North Eastern Railway, Robert Coey obtained a position at Inchicore as a draughtsman. His job would have made him very familiar with McDonnell's standardisation policy and in a good position to assist the successor Aspinall during the four years of that superintendency.

Around this time problems were being found with boiler tubes, at that time mainly brass, in that cracks in their ends were appearing with the attendant leakage and consequent need to take locomotives out of service to repair them. An investigation by the design team eventually traced the trouble to poor annealing treatments of the tube ends, in addition to a somewhat enthusiastic use of the expanders when fitting. The need to ensure adequate quality control was impressed on Coey by this episode. Matters were put into perspective by Aspinall, who carried out a series of experiments on 1861 and 1881 examples of brass tubes: 'All this tends to show that the modern tubes are more readily hardened and rendered brittle'. In other words, the lack of a specialised materials department had lead to the failure to appreciate the variations in materials over the years.

Concurrently, the employment of iron for boilers and frames was being discontinued in favour of steel, now that steel making had been improved by new techniques, of which the Bessemer method was quickly being introduced on a large scale. Up to this time, locomotives had rarely received new boilers when shopped for repairs, but with the steel units capable of accepting higher pressures, the performance advantages confirmed the need for the change of materials.

McDonnell, upon his resignation from the GS&WR, recommended John Aspinall to the Board as his successor. And so, on the 1st November, 1882, Aspinall became the new Locomotive Superintendent. He immediately started by developing the McDonnell class '64' 2-4-0 into the class '52' 4-4-0, four of which were outshopped before 1883 was out. This first batch began the cycle of 4-4-0 design developments to emerge from Inchicore mentioned earlier.

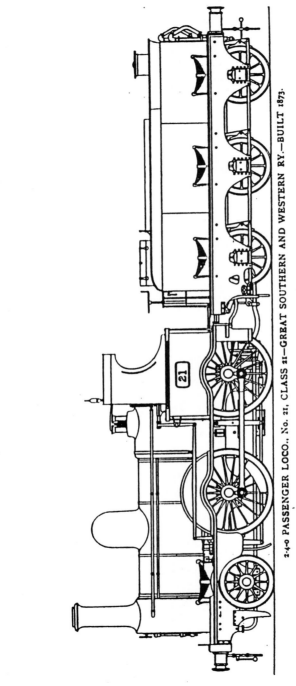

2-4-0 PASSENGER LOCO., No. 21, CLASS 21—GREAT SOUTHERN AND WESTERN RY.—BUILT 1873.

McDonnell class '52' 4-4-0, still in its original condition awaits new duties at Wexford, 9th August, 1935. *R.G. Jarvis*

Some of McDonnell's class '52' were rebuilt with larger boilers. Here No. 12 is found at Inchicore, 4th August, 1936. *J.M. Jarvis*

McDonnell's class '2' small 4-4-0, like its larger brothers of class '52', lived on for many years. No. 10 is here seen at Rosslare, 10th August, 1935.   *J.M. Jarvis*

Class '2' No. 44 sits quietly at Wexford, 1st August, 1936.   *J.M. Jarvis*

McDonnell's passenger 0-4-4T for light work on branches and commuter services. Another long-lived locomotive. At Wexford on 1st August, 1936. *J.M. Jarvis*

The McDonnell 0-6-4T, originally a well and back tank, had acquired side tanks from Coey in the 1890s. Here No. 203 is still on shunting work at Waterford in 1935. Never a very popular type, it was an amalgam of largely standard parts of the 0-4-4T and 0-6-0 class '101'. *J.M. Jarvis*

McDonnell's most famous design, the class '101' 0-6-0. This example No. 134 was built in 1885 by Aspinall, and appears to be ready for a tender-first run from Waterford, 31st July, 1936.

J.M. Jarvis

Not much of the original class '101' would have remained by the time this photograph was taken at Inchicore in 1949. No. 139 was 68 years old then, and sported a Belpaire boiler and extended smokebox together with a new, larger, tender.

J.M. Jarvis

'101' class No. 229, still in largely original condition at Ballycar with a goods for Sligo. No overload here! *Drew Donaldson/Courtesy of Bill Scott*

'101' class No. 184 has been preserved at Inchicore. It was built in 1880, the year Coey started there and still has the original round-topped firebox of the McDonnell's design. Found here at Connelly station, Dublin. *CIE*

John Aspinall, Locomotive Superintendent GS&WR, 1882 to 1886.   *CIE*

Aspinall brought Henry Ivatt up from Cork, where he had been Southern District Superintendent of the GS&WR, as Assistant and Works Manager. As a result, Ivatt and Coey began a 14-year association of close collaboration on design and research matters at Inchicore.

The need to keep abreast of technical advance led Coey to spend much of his spare time preparing for a further degree, again from Queen's College, this time for a Masters in Engineering. This was obtained by submission of an agreed thesis; in 1882, his dissertation was presented and the degree granted.

Shortly after being promoted, Aspinall paid a visit to Crewe to talk with Francis Webb and returned with ideas on developments of steel boilers, compounding and power losses due to slide valve friction, amongst other matters. Aspinall, who was noted for his perception of promising young 'high-flyers', recognised the ability of Robert, 'a keen young engineer', and soon had him and Ivatt hard at work developing a rig and carrying out a series of tests on slide valves to assess the frictional losses attributed to them. Much discussion was taking place in the locomotive fraternity about such losses and it was agreed that a test programme would be of value. Two locomotives were used for the tests carried out, a representative of the class '101' 0-6-0 and a class '52' 4-4-0, fitted with test gear permitting indicator diagrams and valve spindle loads to be measured. The results of the trials showed clearly the effects of adequate lubrication and valve condition on the power requirements to move the valves, on average some 5 hp being absorbed to achieve the required travel. Slide valves were in common use, not to be eclipsed by piston valves for some years yet. It was not long before this ability to manage a comprehensive test programme, coupled with the recently obtained Master's degree, was effectively recognised by Robert's promotion to chief draughtsman. The ladder was being climbed.

By 1885, the slide valve experiments had not produced a design better than the standard valve then in use, and other tasks were crowding in to the design offices. The results were not wasted, however, as they were incorporated into a paper prepared by Coey and Aspinall, 'The Friction of Locomotive Slide Valves', read by Aspinall on 18th December, 1888, at the Institution of Civil Engineers.

In 1885 there was an open competition for the position of County Surveyor in Ireland. Robert, having much experience in the civil engineering sphere from his time with the Port and Docks Board, noticed the request for applicants for this prestigious job. He put his application forward, even though he was well established at Inchicore. Whether he saw considerable advancement prospects or was a little dissatisfied with events on the GS&WR is not known, but he was selected for the job.

However, matters at Inchicore were moving to a change at the top, for John Aspinall was soon to move away to England and the Lancashire & Yorkshire Railway. If Inchicore was to conform to its established rule of replacing the Locomotive Superintendent with his deputy, there would be an opening for a new deputy and Works Manager. Robert was firmly established in a good position and he felt that opportunity beckoned to higher office, from which the ultimate job might come in later years. He therefore declined (or in his own words, 'resigned immediately') the County Surveyor post. This was not to be a backward step, for within a year he was to become Deputy Locomotive Engineer and Works Manager when Aspinall finally resigned in September 1886 to return to England and, ultimately, even greater heights.

Also in 1885, the carriage stock was being updated, with new developments involving convertible seats in the first class carriages provided for the night mail trains. When these seats were turned over they became a full length berth complete with comfortable mattress and pillow. Also, with the Prince and Princess of Wales due to tour Ireland, a Royal Train, consisting of seven carriages, was needed and a flurry of activity saw the works producing the necessary stock. On 13th April this train left Dublin on the tour and passed Inchicore. Many of the workforce conspired to be on duty at a location in the works where the train could be seen passing. Either they wished to try and espy the distinguished passengers or admire their handiwork in the specially prepared locomotive, one of Aspinall's latest 4-4-0s, and the seven gleaming freshly painted and luxuriously appointed carriages. Robert would have had a particularly good view, as the office block was close enough to the main line.

Table One

McDonnell Locomotives (Express and Passenger)

	Class 21	Class 64	Class 52
Type	2-4-0	2-4-0	4-4-0
First batch built	1872	1875	1877
Number constructed	11	12?	6
Cyls (dia. & stroke)	16 in. x 20 in.	17 in. x 22 in.	16 in. x20 in.
Coupled wheels	5 ft 8 in.	6 ft 7 in.	5 ft 8 in.
Leading/bogie wheels	3 ft 9 in.	4 ft 0 in.	3 ft 0 in.
Coupled wheelbase	7 ft 11 in.	7 ft 9 in.	7 ft 11 in.
Total wheelbase (engine)	13 ft 11 in.	14 ft 9 in.	18 ft 8 in.
Boiler barrel length	9 ft 4 in.	9 ft 7 in.	9 ft 4 in.
Boiler dia. (inside)	3 ft 9 in.	4 ft 0 in.	3 ft 9 in.
Firebox length	4 ft 8 in.	5 ft 1 in.	4 ft 8 in.
Grate area	16.0 ft^2	17.5 ft^2	16.0 ft^2
Heating surface, firebox	83.8 ft^2	90.5 ft^2	83.8 ft^2
" " , tubes	770.0 ft^2	843.0 ft^2	770.0 ft^2
" " , TOTAL	853.8 ft^2	933.5 ft^2	853.8 ft^2
Weight, bogie	10 t 0 cwt	10 t 12 cwt	10 t 16 cwt
" , driving	10 t 0 cwt	10 t 16 cwt	10 t 6 cwt
" , trailing	10 t 0 cwt	10 t 6 cwt	10 t 6 cwt
" , TOTAL	30 t 0 cwt	31 t 14 cwt	31 t 8 cwt
Boiler pressure	150lb/in.^{2}	150 lb/in.^{2}	150 lb/in.^{2}
Tractive effort	9,530 lb	10,260 lb	9,530 lb

Chapter Three

Ten Years as Works Manager:
1886-1896

When Aspinall took command at Inchicore, he immediately installed Henry Ivatt as his deputy and Works Manager. We have already seen how Robert Coey was quickly singled out for advancement and so when Ivatt stepped into Aspinall's shoes in 1886 Coey, having shown complete mastery of his job as chief draughtsman, as well as the propensity of a good analytical mind, was promoted to the position vacated by Ivatt.

Robert then prepared to move into 'Mount Vernon', the house provided with the job, once Ivatt had moved to the Locomotive Superintendent's rather sombre but comfortable property, 'St John's', Island Bridge, the garden of which backed onto the railway.

The promotion coincided with Robert's marriage to Elizabeth Amelia Wood, the daughter of a Methodist Minister. They both attended the local Methodist church on a regular basis.

His first task involved completion of the 11 examples of the Aspinall class '60' 4-4-0s still to be turned out. A hand was still kept active on the design side in that, traditionally, Inchicore Works Managers were also expected to deputise for the Locomotive Superintendent and were involved in design discussions at the earliest stages.

The drawing office was initially kept busy by Ivatt and Coey in preparing the designs for a range of tank locomotives. The total fleet at that time consisted of McDonnell 0-4-4T and 0-6-4T types totalling eight in number, plus Aspinall's continuation of the 0-4-4T of which he built 20 from 1883 onwards. The first tank design was for an 0-6-0T, class '207', to replace the rather unsatisfactory 0-6-4Ts. These engines, originally built as rear tanks, placed rather too much weight on the rear bogie reducing that available for adhesion. Also the total wheelbase was considered long, both features a distinct disadvantage for shunting heavy stock in the tight confines of the yards where they were employed. One of these 0-6-4Ts was modified to an 0-4-2T after the rear bogie, frame and rear tank had been removed and the rear coupled wheels had the coupling rods removed. In this guise it was to be employed as a shunting engine at Waterford well into the 20th century, and in fact, appeared on the stock list as an 0-6-0T in 1946! So, at some time, the rear coupling rods had been replaced.

Also on the tank engine front, Ivatt ordered four more examples of the McDonnell class '47' 0-4-4T for branch line work, which were outshopped in 1887.

By now, the stock levels had risen to 176 locomotives, 525 carriages and 3,521 goods vans and wagons, all produced at and serviced by Inchicore works. With a workforce of not more than 1,500 men and boys there was plenty of work for all to repair the stock and produce the new types.

As the locomotive stock was by now in good shape, fully capable of meeting the demands of the current needs, Ivatt turned his attention to some peripheral matters, one of which was the regular meetings required with his first pupil,

Ivatt's first design for the GS&WR was this 0-6-0T for general shunting work to replace the 0-6-4Ts on that work. The latter were prone to derailment in the tight confines of the yards. Here No. 220 is on the transfer goods from Glanmire to Rocksavage (Cork), 26th February, 1957.

Drew Donaldson/Courtesy of Bill Scott

Further batches of the 0-6-0T appeared in 1895, just before Ivatt left for the GNR.

The Locomotive

0-6-0T No. 202 of 1895 takes a rest at Inchicore on 4th August, 1936.   *J.M. Jarvis*

More tank engines appeared under Ivatt. Here No. 35, the 2-4-2T of 1893, which was useful for lighter duties enters Limerick Junction from Limerick on 31st August, 1954.

Drew Donaldson/Courtesy of Bill Scott

When more 2-4-2s were mooted, Ivatt produced the slightly larger 4-4-2T design. Here No. 317 is caught on shed at Limerick Junction, August 1953.   *Drew Donaldson/Courtesy of Bill Scott*

H.A. Ivatt, who gathered his design skills together whilst Locomotive Superintendent at Inchicore 1886-96.   *CIE*

Richard Maunsell. This newcomer to the Inchicore scene was, at that time, attending Trinity College where he was studying for a basic BA degree. The rules of the College in those days allowed students to miss out much of the course work and lectures provided that they sat and passed the exams each year, so he was perfectly in order to take up a pupilship at Inchicore. Richard's father, an eminent Dublin lawyer and JP, had hoped that his son would take a Law degree and be established in the family practice, but his engineering bent had emerged and resulted in Ivatt being approached to consider him as a pupil. The association of Maunsell and Coey in later years was to be of great benefit to the GS&WR as we shall see later.

With almost three years of responsibility for Inchicore under his belt, Coey was put forward for Membership of the Institution of Mechanical Engineers. His application form, dated 15th May, 1889, was proposed by Henry Ivatt and supported by John Aspinall, Alexander McDonnell, Thomas J. Pigot and P. Geoghegan.

Other areas of development involved the production of the first numbers of bogie carriage stock for use on boat and mail trains, following the successful trials of a prototype first and second class composite built the previous year. The majority of the carriage stock still consisted of six-wheeled versions and was to remain so until the early years of the 20th century.

Ivatt kept up his association with matters on the mainland, and in early 1890 attended the inaugural meeting of the reconstituted Association of Railway Locomotive Engineers (ARLE) at the St Pancras Hotel, London. This body was to have regular twice-yearly meetings, at which the latest developments would be discussed and, often, taken back by those present for incorporation into their new designs. At this first gathering the ARLE, which was to have considerable influence on the locomotive scene, accordingly arranged its next meeting to take place in Edinburgh, timed to coincide with the Edinburgh Exhibition of that year. Coey, being left in charge during Ivatt's forays, had plenty of opportunity to get a good feel for the top job which he sensed might come his way if Ivatt moved elsewhere. They were, however, of similar age and so far it looked as if Ivatt was to remain comfortably established in the Dublin environment, which he and his family clearly relished.

The bane of many Locomotive Engineers was the problem of fractures starting in crank axles, which necessitated the replacement of the defective part if noticed during major repairs. Often the slight crack which precipitated matters would go unnoticed, resulting in failure in service. The Inchicore locomotives had, for many years, employed machined forgings for these parts. The basic forging, usually supplied by Messrs Vickers, was machined and finished in the Inchicore machine shop. A few catastrophic failures led Ivatt to instigate a series of tests on samples of crank axles taken from locomotives in service on which incipient cracks were evident. The replacement of such items was costly and lengthy, so it made sense to search for an answer which would lead to reduced maintenance costs.

Accordingly, Coey was instructed to set up a test apparatus to produce vibratory stresses in a crank axle, which Ivatt reasoned would cause the crack to extend until a complete fracture occurred. This indeed happened on the relevant test, but the failure did not occur at the original location of the crack.

INCHICORE WORKS.

Plan of Inchicore Locomotive Carriage and Wagon Works, Great Southern and Western Railway.

I.Mech.E.

(Proceedings Inst. M.E. 1888.)

Inchicore Works in 1888.

Coey designed and built a test rig which suspended the crank axle by its crank pin bearings and was struck on the end of the axle by a concentrated weight. The blows were delivered approximately every 15 seconds, the weight being operated by a cam drive taken from the shop shafting system. This kept the axle in a permanent state of vibration, until failure occurred.

The reasoning behind the set-up was logical. Coey realised that vibration produces repeated high frequency stresses in a stiff material. To ensure that such stresses were applied in a reasonable length of time this approach was needed. In service a crank axle of the type tested would run about 20,000 miles per year, producing some 7,500,000 revolutions or repeat stresses due to the drive forces of the connecting rods. The axle picked for the test had run some 176,000 miles in almost nine years (or 67,500,000 revolutions). To achieve this number of stresses on test in a reasonable time called for a vibratory mode.

The crank axle tested had developed a small four inch crack on the outer web at the corner with the crank pin. This crack grew slowly as the test proceeded, until after about two months a second crack appeared on the inner web, again starting at the corner with the crankpin. This second crack then proceded to grow, the original one not extending any further.

After 645,300 blows catastrophic failure occurred along the inner web. The total time under test was 2,673 hours. This time, at the ordinary shop hours of 54 per week, meant that the experiment lasted almost a full year.

Coey would have paid many a visit to the test rig to check on progress and doubtless was glad when the final failure occurred. Even today, fatigue tests (for this is what the test was) take a long time to complete. The interesting part of the test was that failure did not occur at the position of the original crack.

The method used to induce vibrations in the crank axle was crude and probably not representative of the stresses caused in service. It did, however, indicate that a relatively minor flaw in manufacture could precipitate catastrophic damage. It was also noticeable that all the cracks emanated from, or near, sharp corners in the machined forging. Ivatt and Coey noted that in their opinion a small amount of damage during machining could result in flaws developing. This damage might be as slight as a small scratch caused inadvertently during the final finishing process, or even from a bit of grit trapped in the bearing during assembly.

Although the final report was relatively inconclusive, it did lay the foundation for moves to better manufacturing and assembly quality control. Coey would have instigated these by tightening up on the inspection procedures. The probable cause was mentioned in the closing paragraph of Ivatt's note published in *The Engineer* for 3rd April, 1891 : 'It is borne out by the fact that cracks have been known to start from the corners of small key-seats cut in steel axles.'

Nowadays, we are only too aware of sharp corners acting as stress raisers, such that the tensile stress of the material can be exceeded resulting in a crack commencing, and leading ultimately to complete failure.

The year 1891 brought the birth of Annie, the first of two daughters, who tragically died of meningitis in 1894. Robert and Elizabeth were devastated at the loss of their first child, but their strong Christian faith brought them through what must have been very dark days.

Above: One experimental job in which Coey participated in under Ivatt, was the conversion of Aspinall 4-4-0 No. 93 as a 2-cylinder compound in 1895. It showed no improvement over the simple original and was converted back by Coey in 1902 when new cylinders were required.

The Engineer

Right: The simple, straightforward cab layout of an Aspinall 4-4-0, copied by Ivatt and Coey.

The Engineer

Richard Maunsell completed his degree and pupilship in early 1891, and bade farewell to those at Inchicore, including Coey, who had been his advisers in his time there. Under the Ivatt-Aspinall agreement he was to round off his training at Horwich under Aspinall. He and Robert had always got on very well and their association was to be restored in a few years time when Maunsell returned from India to Inchicore as Works Manager.

The ARLE meeting of 1893 was held at Killarney, with the GS&WR hosting the event. Ivatt and Aspinall reviewed their respective tasks on their constituent railways. The discussed the promising progress of Maunsell, now in charge of the locomotive department at Fleetwood and Blackpool on the Lancashire & Yorkshire Railway, where he had three sheds and a fleet of some 60 locomotives under his control and by all accounts was managing very well in this key posting.

Ivatt still kept in touch with old colleagues at Crewe, his old mentor, Francis Webb, in particular. This, so far as the ARLE was concerned was the missing link, for Webb would not condone such group discussions as were held by that body, yet was happy to talk individually on engineering matters, more especially to ex-Crewe people. It was from this association that the notion of trying out some compounding on the GS&WR emanated, particularly when Ivatt recalled an earlier suggestion by Aspinall for converting the class '60s' to Webb-type compounds. In 1890 Ivatt had ordered Coey to select an 0-6-0 for conversion. The drawing office prepared the necessary schemes and No. 165 of the '101' class was chosen as the guinea-pig. The modified engine obviously showed some promise, as in 1894 a 4-4-0 of class '60', No. 93, received similar treatment. Both had 18 inch cylinders before conversion, changed to 18 inch (high pressure) and 26 inch (low pressure), these sizes and the inside layout being possible due to the Irish 5 ft 3 in. gauge. The compound systems were slightly different for each locomotive in that the 0-6-0 automatically compounded after starting, using a simple valve following Worsdell's principle; the 4-4-0 could be worked simple or compound via a change valve under the driver's control. This was as far as the compound experiment went, both engines eventually reverting to their original condition, the 0-6-0 after the cylinder block cracked in 1896 and the 4-4-0 when called in for major repairs in 1901. Inchicore was really too steeped in its well tried standardisation programme to contemplate adding more components for a limited number of engines. Compounding was only really effective on the longer, faster turns and lost its advantages when employed on the more mundane Irish branch line work, which was typically relaxed. Whilst the experiments had shown no material improvement to be gained from compounding, both Ivatt and Coey were satisfied that neither was there any loss.

Coey had established a good reputation of engineering expertise and judgement with his design team. One particular member of the team at this time was Ernest Joynt, a former pupil of Ivatt and, under Coey in his time as Locomotive Superintendent, to become chief draughtsman. Joynt recalled conversations with Robert on technical matters in glowing terms. Normally economical in his speech, when talking on engineering matters of great interest to himself, Coey could be most eloquent and animated. Ever mindful of the economic interests of the railway company, Robert took a close interest in the progress of work in the shops, to the point of frequent visits to monitor specific jobs which he had ordered. This latter trait sometimes got those involved to move his attention diplomatically to other matters. For example, an urgent job ordered by him was in hand and the chargehand responsible was heard to comment to the foreman: 'For the Lord's sake, try and coax him away and we'll get it done in half the time!'

Despite his apparently unruffled and aloof exterior and clipped Ulster speech, Coey was held in high esteem by the workforce, some of whom discovered a deeply sympathetic nature coupled with a kind heart when personal problems arose. This is perhaps best illustrated in the example given in the next Chapter concerning his handling of Maunsell's return as Works Manager.

Around the middle of 1895, events in England on the Great Northern Railway were shortly to influence matters on the GS&WR at the highest level, and we need now to turn to these in order to progress to the next major shift in Robert Coey's career.

Elizabeth Coey (née Wood), Robert's wife. A photograph taken around 1900.

Anne Parkhill

Chapter Four

The Top Job:
1896-1911

In 1895, the Great Northern Railway Board at King's Cross began to worry about 75-year-old Patrick Stirling's lack of interest in retirement. He showed no sign of stepping out of the position of Locomotive Superintendent. His assistant and Works Manager, Shotton, had died in May of that year, which merely produced a casual remark at the Locomotive Committee meeting the next month regarding the need to consider looking for a replacement; '. . . a man capable of taking over from me in due course.' The Board of the GNR took a more firm line, however, and were certainly determined not to be in a position of having no Locomotive Superintendent. Discreet enquiries were made around the railway scene and, having received a good account of Ivatt's potential from John Aspinall and others, on the 27th August Sir Henry Oakley, the GNR General Manager, accompanied by a fellow Director, R. Wigram, arrived in Dublin to see Ivatt. What they saw obviously pleased them, as upon their return to King's Cross they recommended to the Board that a firm offer be made of the position of Locomotive Superintendent with a guarantee of stepping into Stirling's position upon his retirement, and with the starting date deliberately left open.

Ivatt duly informed the GS&WR Board of this offer. Robert Coey was also taken into his confidence. But the most fascinating train of events was now to take place with regard to the vacancy that would be caused by Coey's elevation from Works Manager if and when Ivatt left. There really was no one at Inchicore suitable for this demanding job, so an outsider would have to be found.

Richard Maunsell was now firmly established as Principal Locomotive Superintendent at Jamalpur, on the East India Railway (EIR), but finding life in India 'a bit slow' and was still looking out for opportunities back in Great Britain or Ireland. Prior to his departure for India he had visited Inchicore to bid farewell to those he had worked with during his pupilship there, Ivatt included. The meeting with Ivatt had brought about the comment that if there was a responsible position at Inchicore, Maunsell would be in a good position to get it.

This comment of Ivatt's had been communicated to John Maunsell, Richard's father, who kept in constant touch with his son, and was additionally well known to some of the Board of the GS&WR, the Chairman, Colvill, in particular. The news of the GNR officers' visit and their choice of Ivatt had been wired to Maunsell in India, who immediately started enquiring of his current employers as to how long it would take to be released from his position with them. His father, meantime, passed on Richard's interest in returning to Inchicore to Colvill, who obviously talked things over with Ivatt. By early October, Ivatt had got to the sticky matter of the salary likely with the Great Northern. Stirling was getting £3,500, a large sum for those days, and the early offer to Ivatt was £1,750, made during a meeting in London with the Chairman of the GNR, the Rt Hon. W.L. Jackson. Ivatt contemplated this verbal offer briefly, then stated that £2,500

Kingsbridge, Dublin.

2ⁿᵈ May 1896

Dear Mr Maunsell —

The Directors have decided not to take their tour this month or next — The 2ⁿᵈ July would be the soonest for starting but probably a little later —

Yours Sincerely

Fra. B. Orchester

Note to Directors regarding a Works Tour

Author's Collection

Inset: R.E.L. Maunsell, Coey's Works Manager for 15 years.

Railway Magazine

would be more like it, and returned to Dublin to await the outcome. This discussion on salaries was communicated to the GS&WR Board and, ultimately to John Maunsell, who wrote to Richard informing him of the salary details. His letter still exists in private hands and emphasises the close relationship John had with Colvill. At the date this letter was written, the 30th October, it seemed likely that Ivatt would stay at Inchicore, as no reply had been received from the GNR. However, three days later a formal offer, at a salary of £2,500, was received by Ivatt, who accepted it two days later, and immediately confirmed his acceptance to Colvill.

John Maunsell, on hearing of this from Colvill, at once cabled to Richard in India, who through his father asked to be considered for the Works Manager job shortly to become vacant. In this he obviously had the backing of Ivatt, plus a good report of steady advancement on the EIR and further support from Aspinall on the L&YR. Then events began to move fast, Stirling died suddenly on 11th November, Ivatt set the date of moving across to Doncaster to be early March 1896, and Richard Maunsell was offered, via his father, the Inchicore Works Manager post. Robert Coey was confirmed as the new Locomotive Superintendent, to commence on 1st March, 1896. These appointments were minuted at a Board meeting on 6th December, 1895.

Upon his instalment as Locomotive Superintendent Robert Coey had a total works force of some 1,600 men and boys and was ultimately responsible for the maintenance and operation of an expanding fleet of locomotives, carriages and goods vehicles. Many of the employees lived in the 147 houses which were built over the years nearby the works. The majority of these houses still stand and continue to be occupied by railway families. For those of the workforce living in the city of Dublin, there were special trains laid on from the Kingsbridge terminus for their benefit.

On 8th March, Richard Maunsell returned to Inchicore to take up the reins in a partnership which lasted for 15 years and saw the works modernised and improved, with a range of new, and sometimes innovative, locomotive designs emerging to enhance the motive power fleet.

There was another reason behind Maunsell's return from India, his engagement to a Miss Edith Pearson, met during his L&YR days. But marriage had been thwarted by a prospective father-in-law who stipulated a specific salary level before he would permit his daughter to wed, such were the rules in the upper middle class society in those days. The Inchicore job provided that salary - plus a free house, and so all objections to the engagement and marriage were withdrawn.

On Saturday 11th April, 1896, the GS&WR employees organised a reception and dinner at the works for their new Superintendent and his Works Manager. Copies of both the menu and programme survive in the author's collection. The menu is a classic example of Victorian plenteousness, seven courses with choices on all except one. The Sunday that followed needed to have been literally a day of rest to complete the digestion of this magnificent repast. Following the dinner, the events began with the toasts to the health of Messrs Coey and Maunsell, followed by congratulatory addresses to each in turn, to which the new Superintendent and his Works Manager replied. Coey's reply has not survived but Maunsell's comprehensive notes for his lengthy response

❧ Menu ❧

Soups.

Jardeniere.   A la Reine.

Fish.

Salmon, Sauce Tartare.
Fillets of Soles, Italian Sauce.

Entrees.

Kromeskys of Oysters.
Mutton Cutlets and Peas.

Joints.

Spring Chicken and Tongue.
Roast Saddle of Mutton.   Sirloin of Beef.

SECOND SERVICE.

Lobster Salad.

Entremets.

Wine Jelly.   Vanilla Cream.
Cabinet Puddings.

Dessert.

Reception programme for Coey and Maunsell

Author's Collection

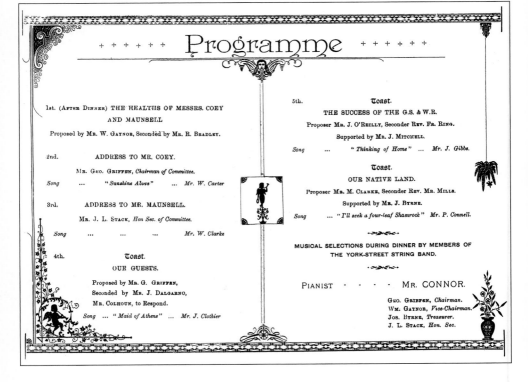

Programme

1st. (AFTER DINNER) THE HEALTHS OF MESSRS. COEY
AND MAUNSELL

Proposed by MR. W. GAYNOR, Seconded by MR. R. BRADLEY.

2nd.   ADDRESS TO MR. COEY.

MR. GEO. GRIFFEN, Chairman of Committee.

Song   ...   "Sunshine Above"   ...   Mr. W. Carter

3rd.   ADDRESS TO MR. MAUNSELL.

MR. J. L. STACK, Hon Sec. of Committee.

Song   ...   .   Mr. W. Clarke

4th.   Toast.
OUR GUESTS.

Proposed by MR. G. GRIFFEN,
Seconded by MR. J. DALGARNO,
MR. COLHOUN, to Respond.

Song   ... "Maid of Athens"   ... Mr. J. Clothier

5th.   Toast.
THE SUCCESS OF THE G.S. & W.R.

Proposer MR. J. O'REILLY, Seconder REV. FR. RING.

Supported by MR. J. MITCHELL.

Song   ...   "Thinking of Home"   ...   Mr. J. Gibbs.

Toast.
OUR NATIVE LAND.

Proposer MR. M. CLARKE, Seconder REV. MR. MILLS.

Supported by MR. J. BYRNE.

Song   ... "I'll seek a four-leaf Shamrock"   Mr. P. Connell.

MUSICAL SELECTIONS DURING DINNER BY MEMBERS OF
THE YORK-STREET STRING BAND.

PIANIST   -   -   -   -   MR. CONNOR.

GEO. GRIFFEN, Chairman.
WM. GAYNOR, Vice-Chairman.
JOS. BYRNE, Treasurer.
J. L. STACK, Hon. Sec.

are in the author's possession. After each address and response the proceedings were enlivened by appropriate songs. There followed no fewer than three more toasting sessions, to the guests, the GS&WR and Ireland, each finishing with yet another song. There was no shortage of talent that night to keep the proceedings well regaled with musical content. The whole affair had been meticulously planned by a committee of 37 drawn from all parts of the works.

Coey had by now moved to the Locomotive Superintendent's house, 'St John's', vacating the one shortly to be occupied by Maunsell and his new bride, who visited Dublin on several occasions to assist Richard in selecting the materials for redecorating this property. Coey had spent much of his spare time setting out the fairly extensive gardens, planting several fruit trees and establishing colourful borders. Edith was also introduced to Coey and his wife, and the families were to become close friends over the years that followed.

One of the key managers at Inchicore, a Mr C.R. Riley, head of the General Stores Department, became a close friend of Robert and frequently visited 'St John's' in a social capacity. A very popular figure within the works, Riley was highly respected in terms of his knowledge, business ability and keen judgement in running the complex department under his control. Close personal relationships such as this aided the smooth, efficient running of the works, and it is clear that Coey placed great reliance on key personnel, such as Riley, that he had come to know on a personal basis.

A little incident illustrating the human side of Robert Coey occurred prior to Maunsell's wedding. A quiet aside to the Company Secretary regarding the forthcoming Directors' tour of the works, which normally required considerable preparation by the Works Manager, resulted in its delay until July, well after the wedding and honeymoon. This also enabled Maunsell to concentrate on the last-minute preparations to the house prior to travelling to London for the nuptials in June.

One little perk of the Locomotive Superintendent's position was the call upon the 'Cab' for transport to and from the works or Dublin. This consisted of an 0-6-0 tank with its own special carriage, and would stop at the bottom of the garden of 'St John's' on the placing of a red flag on the fence. For many years the driver was one Mickey Ramsbottom and, according to contemporary accounts, if the passengers were not waiting upon his arrival, the whistle was put to good use! Robert used the 'Cab' frequently, often being accompanied by his next-door neighbour, a Mr Dent, who from 1903 was to be the General Manager of the GS&WR, on the short trip up to the works or to the Head Office at Kingsbridge station, as business dictated.

The first task awaiting Coey as he settled into his new position was the consideration of the works' modernisation, which he had no hesitation in delegating to Maunsell. The GS&WR was beginning to expand by absorbing smaller concerns, and soon the stock owned by these railways would increase the demands on Inchicore. Maunsell quickly gained a reputation for producing order out of disorder and proved a very popular Works Manager. It had been a long time since Inchicore had had Irishmen in the two top engineering positions, which must have been of great help in the many small matters which arose between workers and management.

Above: The 'Cab', built in 1872 by McDonnell and used for many years by successive Locomotive Superintendents as their personal transport around the GS&WR system.
CIE

Right: Robert Coey in 1896.
CIE

The works' modernisation and expansion programme initiated by Coey and Maunsell consisted firstly of doubling the size of the boiler shop, prior to the installation of a pneumatic plant and a powerful new hydraulic riveter. Extensive reorganisations in the machine shop and smithy took place in the way of modernisation and new equipment. The teamwork benefited from the good relationship between Coey and Maunsell, who had quickly become firm friends both inside and outside the works' environment.

Shortly after taking office, Robert Coey ordered that some experiments be made into the fitting of electric lighting in carriages. Accordingly, some trial installations were made in late 1896 in a few selected vehicles. This was, so far as can be found, the first application in Ireland of this form of lighting on the railways. The pioneer, so far as railways in England were concerned, was the 1881 installation in a Pullman car by the London, Brighton & South Coast Railway. For this application accumulators were used, which required charging at Victoria. This meant that for some of the time this carriage was not available for service and probably caused the experiment to fail because of the restricted stock availability.

Together with the top job came the offer of membership of the Association of Railway Locomotive Engineers, Robert first attending their 27th November, 1896, meeting at the St Pancras Hotel in London. Both Aspinall and Ivatt were present to congratulate Coey on his election, and among others attending were William Dean, S.W. Johnson, James Holden, T. Hurry Riches, William Worsdell and Matthew and James Stirling, the latter the current President. The business of this particular meeting consisted of lengthy discussions on carriage sheds, wagon brakes and fog signalling in addition to the sharing of thoughts on locomotive developments.

One extra, but often worrying, task falling Coey's way now he had risen to the top, was the need to deal with the growing move to trade unionism within the works. The earliest engineering trade union in Ireland is recorded as the Amalgamated Society of Engineers (ASE), established in Dublin in 1851, at the same time as its foundation in England. However, it was not until 1894 that conditions at Inchicore permitted a branch of the ASE to be formed there. Robert, as Works Manager, would have been drawn into the negotiations for this event. The relatively small (80 members) branch quickly became the catalyst for further branches throughout the GS&WR network. Matters dealt with would have been working hours and conditions, discrimination disputes, promotions and company policy covering security of employment.

The fact that no serious strike occurred until 1902 bears testimony to Coey's and Maunsell's capable handling of matters where unions were concerned, being well backed up by their immediate staff. This 1902 strike lasted from 23rd May until 9th October and brought the works almost to a standstill, despite the employment of a temporary labour force. The core of the dispute was a demand for a 3s. (15p) increase in the basic wage. It was this dispute that caused the reversion to outside contractors for the supply of new locomotives as we shall see in later Chapters.

Having fully recovered from their 1894 tragedy with Annie, Robert and Elizabeth were overjoyed with the arrival of Maud in 1901. As outgoing and

Inchicore works as will be found today looking to the West. Apart from the modern rebuild of the running shed of the 1950s, the layout of the main works is substantially as in Coey's time. Across the other side of the railway, however, things have changed dramatically from open countryside to extensive housing estates and light industry.

CIE

Left: Inchicore works, the machine shop.
Railway Magazine

Right: Inchicore works, the smithy.
Railway Magazine

Left: Inchicore works, the office block. Note the old Bury 2-2-2 on plinth. *Railway Magazine*

Right: Railway houses outside Inchicore works.
Railway Magazine

cheerful as her father was withdrawn and serious, Maud, who never married, was a welcome late addition who devoted her life to caring for her parents in the later years of their lives. In her early years she was cared for by a series of Irish nurserymaids who, on Sundays, when her parents were attending the Methodist church nearby, often took her with themselves to the nearby Catholic Church. These church attendances had a lasting effect on Maud, for in her later days she recalled the effect this had on her choice of church as she grew up. She recounted finding the Catholic church 'so bright and colourful' with its flamboyant decoration. When living in England later on she was to be drawn to attending a very high Anglican church, with its similarities in decor and ritual to that of the Catholic church.

Richard and Edith Maunsell had, two years previously, themselves rejoiced at the safe arrival of their daughter Netta.

Ivatt and Aspinall visited Dublin several times as they still had happy memories of their days spent there. Maud, in later years, recalled the friendship between her parents and Ivatt in the early years of the century. It is also on record that Aspinall and his daughter Edith visited the Maunsells in 1898 and no doubt they would have paid their respects to the Coeys.

Inchicore, under the leadership of Coey and Maunsell, improved its efficiency and productivity considerably, and this was to benefit the railway in the near future as the GS&WR became the predominant line in Ireland both in terms of track mileage and area coverage. We need now to examine how Robert Coey and his team attacked the needs of this expanding company for locomotive and rolling stock, which in the context of carriages was shortly to require a further expansion of bogie stock and the introduction of corridor gangways in line with other developments across the Irish Sea.

Steam hammer in the smithy, with the crew and foreman.   *CIE*

Chapter Five

The Express Locomotives: 1900-1911

One feature which had a retrograde effect on Coey's express locomotives was the need to keep to a 16 ton axle loading so that these engines were not restricted in route availability. The relaxation of this limit in the early years following Coey's retirement produced the catalyst for the rebuilding programmes initiated on the 4-4-0s, largely revolving around reboiling and frame strengthening. The earlier versions with parallel boilers suffered from shortage of steam in certain conditions, due to the limited boiler size dictated by the axle load restriction. Hence the early improvements in firebox size, as we shall see.

In 1896, when Coey took command, the mainstay of the GS&WR express locomotives were the Aspinall class '52' and class '60', both 4-4-0s. The latter was actually a development of the former, which was itself derived from the McDonnell class '64' 2-4-0. A total of 20 class '52' and 15 class '60' were in service at that time.

As the turn of the century approached, the introduction of bogie stock on the major expresses resulted in a large increase in train weights. For example, the Dublin and Queenstown day mail trains, originally 90 tons of six-wheeled stock were now 190 tons of 50 ft bogie stock. Additionally, around 1898, dining cars and longer 60 ft corridor stock appeared, pushing train weights up to 250 tons or more on occasions. The Aspinall 4-4-0s were beginning to struggle with the 190 ton loads, and frequently required double-heading on the 250 ton trains, not an efficient or economic way of handling matters. The catalyst was there for Coey to apply his expertise in the form of new and more powerful express types.

The 4-4-0 had been the archetypal express locomotive in the British Isles for several decades,and was to remain so for some years to come. So it was logical for this classic layout to be continued.

Coey took time properly to assess the situation before launching a comprehensive programme of development in which the Aspinall designs were to be superseded by locomotives of greater capability in terms of hauling power and efficiency.

And so, in 1899, the drawings were produced for the first of a range of new classes of 4-4-0s, which were outshopped in 1900 as class '301'. This first batch of new engines were given names, a departure from the normal practice:

301	Victoria	-	after the Queen.
302	Lord Roberts	-	of Boer War fame
303	Saint Patrick	-	as befits the country of origin
304	Princess Ena	-	as Princess Ena of Battenberg had recently visited Inchicore Works

A completely new departure in styling of the running plate, changes in the motion and cylinders, and the final farewell to the oven-type double smokebox doors on express types were the main changes wrought by Coey. The firebox

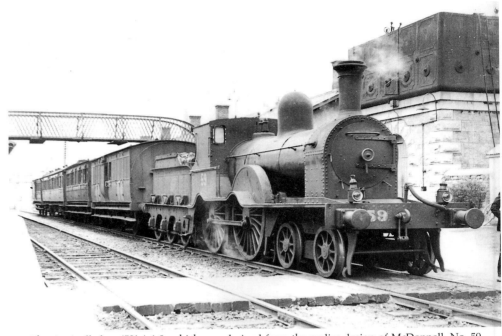

The Aspinall class '52' 4-4-0, which was derived from the earlier design of McDonnell. No. 59 still going strong in 1952 at Tuam.   *Drew Donaldson/Courtesy of Bill Scott*

Robert Coey's first 4-4-0, the class '301' of 1900.   *John Alsop Collection*

top stays were of the radial type in place of the girder and sling type used previously. The splashers were completely remodelled, with the final product looking very like the Wainwright 'D' on the South Eastern & Chatham Railway (SE&CR). The first two had piston valves, but these were replaced early on by the slide valves of the other two examples.

Initially, the class '301' proved a poor steamer, and so Coey ordered a series of tests to be made using different chimneys and blastpipes to improve the draughting. Richard Maunsell was heavily involved in these tests and the importance of good draughting was impressed upon him. This impression which stayed with him, as was witnessed in the generally excellent steaming characteristics associated with many of his designs later for the SE&CR and Southern.

A further innovation on this class was the fitting of smoke deflectors to the chimneys, but their effectiveness was not sufficient to warrant their retention. The new, larger, splashers soon had semi-circular openings cut in their sides to ease the oiling of axle-boxes and coupling rod pins. To improve the steaming qualities further the fireboxes were eventually replaced by new ones having wider water spaces, which also helped reduce repair costs.

Starting with this batch, new tenders of 3,345 gallon capacity were supplied, subsequently becoming the standard tender for all future Coey locomotives. The early 4-4-0s were immediately rostered for the Dublin-Cork expresses, and would probably have sped Robert's parents to and from Cork on their visits to his sister Mary and her husband Robert Parkhill, a businessman of some standing in that city.

Once the early problems had been resolved the class '301' proved very useful in service, yet Coey was not completely satisfied with his initial foray into the 4-4-0 scenario. So a follow-on order was placed for a further four in 1902 which would have improved steaming qualities. These had increased firebox size and formed the class '305'. The boiler centre-line was raised four inches and balanced slide valves employing Richardson's strips were introduced. There was a slight problem associated with leaking tubes caused by the firebox flexing. This was traced to the use of radial stays, and remedial action put in hand.

Prior to the class '305', studies had been ordered by Coey into a derivative employing a higher boiler pressure of 175 psi, in addition to a Belpaire firebox. It seems that soon after the introduction of the class '301' Robert realised the shortcomings in steaming still needed some attention. This design was never approved, and the 175 psi pressure had to wait until Maunsell adopted it in 1912 for his class '341', whilst the Belpaire box first appeared on the class '368' 2-6-0 in 1909. Whilst wishing to adopt new design features, Coey appeared constrained by the need to keep as many standard parts as possible in the interests of economy. Perhaps his natural quiet ways were not amenable to making a strong case for new features involving extra costs in new tooling. There were, however some areas where he did have his say enough to ensure that technology was not ignored. A good theoretical man, he could make a convincing argument for experimentation on many occasions.

Superheating was by now becoming close to being a reality, and many CMEs were beginning to experiment with it. Robert Coey commenced his application

The class '305' improvement on the '301', built in 1902.   *The Locomotive*

The class '305' was subject to several experimental changes. This depicts the taper boiler fitted in 1905.   *The Locomotive*

in 1902 with a modification to class '60' 4-4-0 No. 62, which was fitted with a smokebox superheater, or 'steam dryer'. Only a moderate degree of superheating was achieved, but this was sufficient to dry the steam such that increased wear of the slide valves occurred. This negated any economy in working by causing increased maintenance costs. The experiment was terminated after six months and the mass of complex tubing removed from the smokebox, where it had probably caused some draughting difficulties hardly conducive to good steaming.

One small test programme, involving No. 307 of class '305' in 1904, was the installation of a novel valve gear developed by James Marshall. This was manufactured and installed for comparitive trials. The test train involved both Coey and Maunsell, Coey on the engine and Maunsell on the train to monitor readings. The results of the trials showed no marked improvement over the existing valve gear, and the locomotive eventually reverted to its original condition, but at least this showed that Robert was always ready to experiment. It is perhaps worth noting that some results of this test on the Marshall gear are recorded in *The Engineer* for 1905, and analysis of this (*see Appendix*) has shown the Coey class '305' well up in terms of power output when compared with similar locomotives on other British railways at that time. This was not to be the end of the experiment, for later a slightly improved version of Marshall's gear was fitted to No. 332 of the class '321'. This locomotive operated satisfactorily for some years with this gear, but any further adoption was thwarted by Robert's retirement. The locomotive continued in modified form through Maunsell's reign and it fell to Maunsell's successor, Watson, to order the removal of the Marshall gear when No. 332 came in for rebuilding.

Train weights now looked like increasing far beyond that envisaged, as mentioned earlier, with even classes '301' and '305' likely to be at the limit of their capacity soon. Typical Dublin-Cork mail trains comprised seven bogies (about 180 tons) plus three or four extra coaches for slipping at Kildare, 30 miles from Dublin, a total starting weight of 250 tons. This initial load was close to the limit of the Aspinall class '60' up the bank from Kingsbridge. With the class '301' in service and the class '305' appearing in traffic the load sometimes could rise to more than 300 tons, one typical formation being seven bogies plus nine 6-wheelers and two vans. Clearly even greater power was needed to ensure that time was to be kept as loads increased. A further improved design in 1903, to become class '310', was schemed in the drawing office. The extra effort came from an increase in cylinder size from 18 in. to 18½ in. and a corresponding 2 sq. ft increase in grate area over the 21 sq. ft of class '305'. Robert had obviously taken note of Ivatt's dictum regarding the measure of the power of a locomotive being 'its capacity to boil water' whilst reading the Proceedings of the Institution of Mechanical Engineers. The discussion that followed a paper given by Sauvage on French locomotives in June 1900 contained this statement. Clearly, a larger grate area made this possible, on two grounds, the increased heating surface and the larger fire.

The improvements made on the class '310' 4-4-0s proved very successful, they were proving good steamers, yet Robert still thought about even more power being required soon. The extra tractive effort of the class '310s' enabled brisk starts up the awkward gradients at Kingsbridge and Glanmire Road to be the

The class '321' started with taper boilers after the successful use on the class '305'. No. 329 still sports this after the first rebuild of 1912 with superheater.
National Railway Museum

norm rather than the exception, as had been the case with the lighter, less powerful, McDonnell, Aspinall and earlier Coey 4-4-0s. Coey clearly had found the right answer in his approach to the express scene. However, he also realised that further improvements lay around the corner and resolved to examine and select those he thought would benefit his future 4-4-0 developments. Much discussion around these developments took place, with Maunsell and Joynt in particular. Maunsell was to be influenced by these deliberations, and his own 4-4-0 developments in later years were given a solid foundation to build on by these happenings at Inchicore in the early years of the 20th century.

Owing to a long strike of fitters and turners all locomotive building at Inchicore was stopped in 1903. The six new engines of class '310' were ordered from Neilson, Reid & Co., Glasgow, shortly to become part of the North British Locomotive Company. Delivered in late 1903, these were the most powerful express types to run on the GS&WR to date.

Still requiring improved steaming capability, Coey then introduced the taper boiler to the Irish scene. He had visited North America in 1903 for reasons to be explained in the next Chapter, and had seen the developments in such boilers instigated there. Realising the considerable increase in heating surface possible with such an arrangement he soon had Joynt at work scheming a taper boiler to update one of the class '310' for trials. The engine was transformed into an excellent steamer, always having adequate steam on demand for even the heaviest train, so it was fundamental that the next batch of 4-4-0s (class '321') ordered in 1904, had tapered boilers. Twelve were turned out between 1904 and 1906, such was the success of this design change. Up to now, only Churchward on the Great Western had shown any interest in this aspect of locomotive design, so Coey was well up to current practice on that railway.

By 1906, more 4-4-0s were required to cope with the increasing frequencies of the express services. The tapered boiler was by now being fitted to all the class '305s' and so, with 16 examples of technically advanced steam producers in service and proving very successful, it was logical that the next batch also employed that boiler. Eight of class '333' were built, essentially similar to the earlier class '305' as reboilered, with much of the motion interchangeable, but with one significant difference in that the coupled wheels were 5 ft 8½ in. compared to the 6 ft 7 in. standard up to now. This had a considerable effect on tractive effort, which was now 17,100 lb., a marked increase on the earlier types. Four were outshopped in 1907, followed by a second four in 1908. This latter batch had one significant difference in that the bogies were redesigned to have outside bearings. The original 3 ft diameter wheels with inside bearings tended to run hot at high speeds. The weight taken by this bogie, previously employed on the Aspinall 4-4-0s had increased from 13 t. 10 cwt of the class '60' to 18 t. 4 cwt of the '333', but probably this was just part of the problem, the main reason apparently being poor lubrication of the journal pads. All Coey's other 4-4-0s employed 3 ft 6 in. bogie wheels with the consequent reduction in rotational speeds. The class '333' had one further claim to fame, this being the provision of another batch of four in 1936, some two years after their designer's death. Not many locomotive designers have been accorded that honour, even the long-lived class '101s' were all produced within Alexander McDonnell's lifetime.

The Coey class '333' 4-4-0, with smaller driving wheels. No. 340, of the second batch, is in original condition here. *National Railway Museum*

Some class '333s' were built in the 1930s long after their designer's demise. Here No. 345 of that batch is at Inchicore Shed on 24th September, 1949. *J.M. Jarvis*

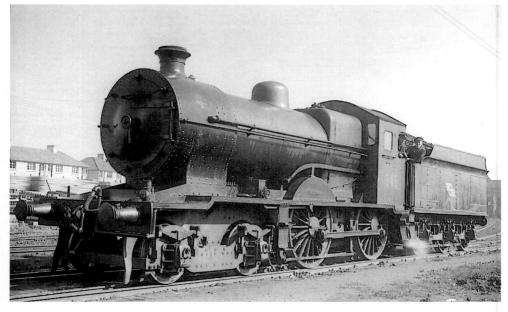

November 1907 saw a 4-6-0 express design submitted to the Board for consideration. Although no diagram of this has survived, it probably was an express version of the class '362' goods locomotive. R.N. Clements, with the available evidence did actually draw out what he thought could pass as this design, but the boiler pitch would, he estimated, have been at least 9 ft 3 in., very high for the day. However, the poor performance of the class '362' probably killed this one off, and the proposal lapsed.

The class '333' were put into service on the Cork to Rosslare boat expresses, involving several sharp gradients of 1 in 70 but the new 4-4-0s tackled these easily, pulling eight or more coaches with, sometimes, up to seven or eight parcels vans. Other trains which involved frequent stops on tight schedules also benefited by the excellent accelerative capabilities of these locomotives.

Robert Coey had, over a few years, developed his own brand of 4-4-0 express engine into 34 examples of modern and efficient types for all the major express and fast passenger trains. These engines, whilst rebuilt in later years, were to last the Irish railways until almost the end of steam some 50 years hence, although cascaded down to secondary services as new 2-6-0s and 4-6-0s appeared after the early 1920s.

By 1909, Coey's health was beginning to affect matters, in that around this time he spent several lengthy periods off work. Richard Maunsell stepped into the breach; their teamwork at Inchicore was legendary.

We have seen that Coey was a man of few words, yet meticulous about detail not only in the design offices but on the shop floor as well. Whilst on the outside giving an impression of calm orderliness, he continually worried about schedules and economics. This took a toll on his health and he was beset with attacks of migraine accentuated by stress. All too often we read about illness of those in high places induced by attention to details normally considered now to be outside their remit. Management styles in the early years of the 20th century were still very much of the Victorian era. The higher a person rose, they tended to retain responsibilities which should have been delegated and the workload grew as a result, as did their age. The pressure became relentless and only the very robust could weather this with no immediate effect.

Robert Coey was, unfortunately, one whose constitution was not strong enough to permit his withstanding the pressures of a heavy responsibility as time moved on. This eventually cut short his career, as we shall see. However, he did manage to delegate some of his large workload to his very capable assistant, as he could rely absolutely on Richard Maunsell's expertise in times of need.

One of the tasks which devolved onto Maunsell concerning the class '321' locomotives was the fitting of a superheater. Superheating was becoming established as an effective way of improving locomotive economy and performance. Such developments did not pass Coey by and he obtained approval to install a Schmidt type superheater to one engine for comparitive trials. No. 326 was selected for these trials and the cylinders increased in diameter to 20 inches, to take advantage of the greater expansive qualities of superheated steam. The tractive effort was thus increased to 17,900 lb., an addition of 2,580 lb.

Table Two

Express 4-4-0s in Coey's Time

Designer	Aspinall	Aspinall	Coey	Coey	Coey	Coey	Coey
Class	52	60	301	305	310	321	333
First batch built	1883	1885	1900	1902	1903	1904	1907
Number constructed	20	15†	4	4	6	12	8
Cyls (dia. and stroke)	17 in. x 22 in.	18 in. x 24 in.	18 in. x 26 in.	18 in. x 26 in.	18 in. x 26 in.	18 in. x 26 in.	18 in. x 26 in.
Coupled wheels	6 ft 7 in.	6 ft 7 in.	6 ft 7 in.	6 ft 7 in.	6 ft 7 in.	6 ft 7 in.	5 ft 8½ in.
Bogie wheels	3 ft 0in.	3 ft 0 in.	3 ft 6 in.	3 ft 6 in.	3 ft 6 in.	3 ft 6 in.	3 ft 0 in.
Coupled wheelbase	7 ft 9 in.	8 ft 3 in.	8 ft 6 in.	8 ft 6 in.	9 ft 0 in.	9 ft 0 in.	8 ft 6 in.
Total wheelbase (engine)	19 ft 5 in.	20 ft 5 in.	21 ft 8 in.	21 ft 8 in.	22 ft 2 in.	22 ft 2 in.	21 ft 8 in.
Boiler barrel length	9 ft 7 in.	9 ft 9 in.	10 ft 4 in.	10 ft 4 in.	10 ft 4 in.	10 ft 4 in.	10 ft 4 in.
Boiler dia. (inside)	4 ft 0 in.	4 ft 3 in.	4 ft 6 in.	4 ft 6 in.	4 ft 5¾ in.	5 ft 0½ in.*	5 ft 0½ in.*
Firebox length	5 ft 1 in.	5 ft 5 in.	5 ft 10 in.	6 ft 0½in.	6 ft 6½ in.	6 ft 6½ in.	6 ft 0½ in.
Grate area	17.5 ft²	18.8 ft²	20.4 ft²	21 ft²	23 ft²	23 ft²	21 ft²
Heating surface, firebox	96 ft²	112.5 ft²	120 ft²	127 ft²	135.25 ft²	128.1 ft²	128.1 ft²
" ", tubes	835 ft²	938 ft²	1,100 ft²	1,148 ft²	1,110ft²	1,283.9 ft²	1,283.9 ft²
" ", TOTAL	931 ft²	1050.5 ft²	1,220ft²	1,275 ft²	1,245.3 ft²	1,412 ft²	1,412 ft²
Weight, bogie	11 t 18 cwt	13 t 10 cwt	16 t 14 cwt	17 t 14 cwt	17 t 12 cwt	18 t 11 cwt	18 t 4 cwt
" ", driving	12 t 8 cwt	12 t 18 cwt	14 t 16 cwt	14 t 6 cwt	16 t 0 cwt	16 t 14 cwt	16 t 0 cwt
" ", trailing	12 t 2 cwt	12 t 17 cwt	13 t 4 cwt	14 t 16 cwt	15 t 18 cwt	16 t 16 cwt	15 t 18 cwt
" ", TOTAL	36 t 8 cwt	39 t 5 cwt	44 t 14 cwt	46 t 16 cwt	49 t 10 cwt	52 t 1 cwt	50 t 2 cwt
Boiler pressure	160 psi	140 psi	160 psi	160 psi	160 psi	160 psi	160 psi
Tractive effort	10,950 lb.	11,710 lb.	14,500 lb.	14,500 lb.	15,320 lb.	15,320 lb.	17,100 lb.

* Tapered boiler, diameter quoted is maximum
† 11 of this number built under Ivatt between 1886 and 1895.

The class '333s' were rebuilt with Belpaire fireboxes/boilers in the 1920s. Here No. 339, ex-Amiens Street, passes Shanganagh Junction on 4th May, 1957.

Drew Donaldson/Courtesy of Bill Scott

Another 1936-built class '333', No. 342, at Pallas on 31st October, 1955. These were popular locomotives.   *Drew Donaldson/Courtesy of Bill Scott*

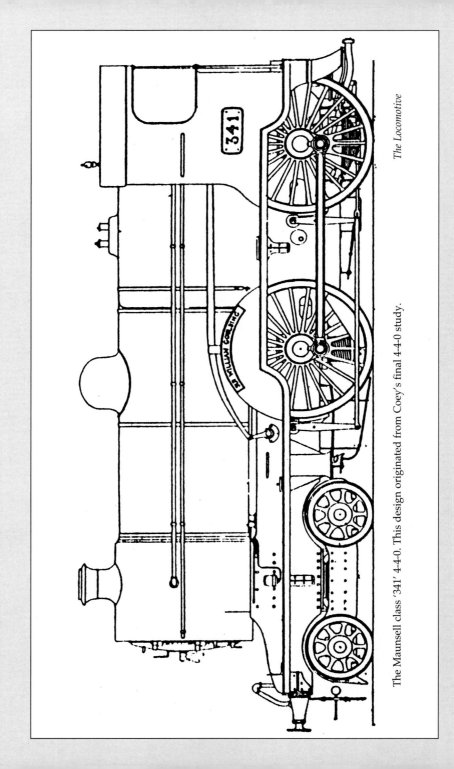

The Maunsell class '341' 4-4-0. This design originated from Coey's final 4-4-0 study.

The Locomotive

One final 4-4-0 development was to be started before the ill-health brought about Robert's early retirement, this being the scheming of what was to become class '341' under Maunsell. To qualify this it is necessary to go back and recap on some earlier work of Coey. Although the final GS&WR 4-4-0 is attributed to Richard Maunsell, it really was the culmination of a series of project studies carried out by Coey. Maunsell, in his rôle of deputy to Robert, would have been kept informed of these studies and may well have had temporary charge over them during Coey's frequent absences, particularly as his retirement approached.

The first clues as to the final outcome in terms of design geneology may be found as far back as the 1901 study, mentioned earlier, which introduced two features to become part of the No. 341 final iteration, namely a Belpaire firebox and 175 psi boiler pressure. It has been suggested that the abortive 1901 study was an attempt to offer one answer to the steaming problems associated with the class '301'. However, in the interests of standardisation, the next production engines were, we have seen, the class '305' derivatives of the 301.

The other 4-4-0 developments plus all the goods and tank locomotive developments carried out until 1909 meant little time could be spent on looking into any meaningful new approach for an express 4-4-0. Not until late 1910 did any more project work materialise, this in the form of a development of the class '321'. The limited amount of evidence on this 1910 study indicates a class '321' with a longer wheelbase to accommodate a longer boiler. So far as is known, the firebox was the standard round-top affair.

By the next study, in early 1911, a further lengthening of the wheelbase had taken place together with a very large diameter (for Inchicore) boiler, of some 5 ft 4 in. The small net increase in total weight of some 1¼ tons appears optimistic for such a large boiler and places doubt on the weight estimates for this and the previous design. The Belpaire firebox reappeared in this study. However, the cylinder size was increased to 20 in. diameter from the earlier 18½ in., to account for the large boiler.

Four months later, as retirement approached for Coey, a further iteration lengthened the wheelbase by one inch, reduced the boiler to 5 ft 2⅛ in., and the smokebox was extended, but no superheater was proposed at this stage. This latter suggests that superheating was to be considered as a future development. The total heating surface of 1,808 sq. ft is approaching that of No. 341.

Retirement was now imminent, so it is around this and the final study we find the influence of the new Locomotive Superintendent appearing. The boiler size and provision for superheating was evidence of Maunsell's thinking as to 4-4-0 developments. Grate area had increased to almost 25 sq. ft and all was set for the final study which was turned out as Robert Coey left Inchicore, and subsequently Dublin, for quieter times in England.

When one compares the details of the July 1911 design with those of No. 341, we see that here we have essentially that express development of Richard Maunsell, who stamped his authority on it by restyling the cab and running plate and ensured that a superheater was installed as standard. We know that No. 341 also employed Walschaerts valve gear, but exactly when this appeared during the series of studies is unknown, more probably near the end. Coey had long been an exponent of the Stephenson gear.

Table Three

The Evolution of No. 341

	25.02.01	15.11.10	24.01.11	01.05.11	01.07.11	Notes
Date						
Cyls (dia. and stroke)	18 in. x 26 in.	18½ in. x 26 in.	20 in. x 26 in.	20 in. x 26 in.	20 in. x 26 in.	(1) The July 1911 design was the baseline for Maunsell's class '341'. The changes introduced by Maunsell were limited to styling of running plate and cab, sufficient for the final locomotive to be distinctive enough in looks to signify a different designer at work.
Coupled wheels	6 ft 7 in.	6 ft 7 in.	6 ft 7 in.	6 ft 7 in.	6 ft 7 in.	
Bogie wheels	3ft 6in.	3 ft 6 in.	3 ft 0 in.	3 ft 0 in.	3 ft 0 in.	
Coupled wheelbase	9 ft 0 in.	9 ft 6 in.	9 ft 10 in.	9 ft 11 in.	9 ft 11 in.	
Total wheelbase	22 ft 5 in.	22 ft 11 in.	23 ft 8 in.	23 ft 2 in.	23 ft 2 in.	
Boiler length	11 ft 0½ in.	11 ft 0 in?	11 ft 0 in.	11 ft 0 in.	11 ft 4¾ in.	(2) The superheater appears in July as a standard fit. Coey had clearly approved its inclusion, probably one of the final decisions to be made before he retired from the scene.
Boiler dia.	4 ft 5¾ in.	n/a	5 ft 4 in.	5 ft 2⅝ in.	5 ft 2⅝ in.	
Firebox type	Belpaire	Round	Belpaire	Belpaire	Belpaire	
Firebox length	?	7 ft 0 in.	7 ft 0 in.	7 ft 0 in?	7 ft 0 in.	
Grate area		?	?	24.8 ft²	24.8 ft²	(3) All these designs would have had the standard Inchicore tender of 3,345 gallon capacity and 37½ tons laden weight. The final estimated weight for the definitve class '341' was therefore in the region of 97 tons. Future Maunsell 4-4-0s were not to this weight until the advent of the 'L1' on the Southern in 1926.
Heating surface, (firebox)	131 ft²	?	?	156 ft²	155.7 ft²	
" " , (tubes)	1,278 ft²	?	?	1,652 ft²	1,364.9 ft²	
" " , (s/heater)	-	-	-	?	335.1 ft²	
" " , (Total)	1,409 ft²	?	?	1,808 ft²	1,855.7 ft²	
Weight (bogie)	?	18 t 10 cwt	18 t 15 cwt	?	21 t 17 cwt	
" (drivers)	?	18 t 0 cwt	18 t 10 cwt	?	18 t 15 cwt	
" (Trailing)	?	18 t 0 cwt	18 t 10 cwt	?	18 t 15 cwt	
" (Total)	49 t 0 cwt	54 t 10 cwt	55 t 15 cwt	?	59 t 7 cwt	
Boiler press	175 psi	160 psi	160 psi	160 psi	175 psi	
Tractive Effort	15,860 lb.	15,320 lb.	17,900 lb.	17,900 lb.	19,580 lb.	

Coey 4-4-0s were long-lived. Here class '321' No. 328, in rebuilt guise, heads a special train for the Papal Envoys visiting Ireland in the 1950s. The train consists of a guard's brake/baggage van, dining car, ex-GS&WR state saloon No. 351 and ex-MGWR 12-wheeled state saloon. The last two coaches were built in 1903 for the Royal train used by King Edward VII on his tour of Ireland in that year. Note the tidy crew, collars and ties with neat peaked caps. The bowler-hatted gentleman on the footplate will be the Inspector riding the train. Inchicore works is in the background complete with Victorian gas lamps. This view gives a good impression of Sancton Woods' castellated architecture for the original running shed.

CIE

Although No. 341 has always been listed as a Maunsell locomotive, we see that it was a logical development of Coey's 4-4-0s. It says much for the rapport between Coey and Maunsell that the latter merely restyled the resulting locomotive, being happy to leave the sound engineering of Coey relatively untouched. Table Three summarises these 4-4-0 developments from data currently available.

However, weight control still eluded the design team and when No. 341 appeared, the route restriction was just as predicted. The subsequent fate of what was to be a one-off is recorded elsewhere. The Maunsell brand of styling and cab was adopted years hence when the other Coey 4-4-0s were rebuilt, and which he took with himself to the SE&CR in 1913.

The only criticism one can level at the express locomotive developments initiated under Coey was the lack of a 4-6-0 design. It probably would have been better to press for a 4-6-0 on the grounds of keeping the axle loading to a reasonable figure whilst permitting a larger boiler/firebox combination with a sizeable increase in heating surface. However, the cost of such a design probably weighed against its introduction at that time. Also, we shall see that the goods 4-6-0s were not particularly successful locomotives and their uninspiring performance may have influenced the Board's deliberations on funding a 4-6-0 express type. 4-4-0s, in general, are free-running types and are capable of negotiating the continuous sharp curves abounding on some lines. The 4-6-0 would suffer from increased flange wear due to the longer coupled wheelbase and it is clear that such matters would have been discussed by Coey, Maunsell and Joynt at some stage. This analysis was to reappear in Maunsell's days on the Southern Railway, when a new design for the Hastings line expresses was being formulated. Tests on 2-6-0s showed high flange wear over this route with its tight curves, and recourse to a 4-4-0 produced the famous 'Schools' class, the ultimate in this classic layout.

This, then, covers the express developments on the GS&WR attributed to Robert Coey. His design expertise provided a legacy of efficient, long-lived and reliable locomotives which served that railway and its successors for many years. We need now to assess the goods situation and how Coey tackled this increasingly important side of the GS&WR operation.

An immaculate No. 301 in CIE service, well over 50 years old and still going strong on 12th June, 1953.   *J.M. Jarvis*

Chapter Six

Goods and Tank Locomotives:
1898-1911

Whilst the passenger scene was to be transformed within four or five years of Robert's installation as Locomotive Superintendent, the goods locomotive stock consisted mainly of a large fleet of McDonnell 0-6-0's, class '101'. This design had been progressively updated as each batch was produced and the class had reached a total of 91 examples by 1896, including the two authorised in the last days of Ivatt's time.

The class '101', an 1867 design, was a sound and durable type and, although credited to McDonnell, contemporary records state that the origin of the 'Standard Goods', as it was called, was actually attributable to Beyer, Peacock. That company, in fact, supplied two of the first batches totalling six engines in 1867-8 from a set of requirements, and presumably drawings, supplied by Inchicore. However, it has been suggested that the class 101 is a pure Beyer, Peacock design, based on its 0-6-0 supplied by that company to the Danube and Black Sea Railway whilst McDonnell was employed there as Locomotive Superintendent. In that case the Inchicore drawings would probably have been simple line diagrams only accompanying a general specification. There were four 0-6-0s built at Inchicore prior to the Beyer, Peacock batches, but these are labelled the 'hybrids' and were constructed of parts salvaged from withdrawn types. Successive rebuilds of these four incorporated many standard parts drawn from class '101' stocks, until they were, to all intents and purposes, so similar to the true class '101' that they were classified as such. Furthermore, the fact that the '101s' were a Beyer, Peacock design is confirmed by the knowledge that this company supplied two to the Dublin and Belfast Junction Railway, in 1872, which were identical to those supplied to Inchicore.

Coey continued to add to this fleet, four each in 1898, 1899 and 1902 and eight in 1903, with only minor differences. He saw no reason to supersede a proven and reliable design with something new and untested. The '101s' were capable of travelling over most of the GS&WR's mileage due to the low axle loading of some 12 tons. Having all their weight available for adhesion, they could manage freight trains of 500 tons, equivalent to 45 wagons, which at that time was more than adequate. Economical to service and repair and seemingly insensitive to coal quality, the '101s' coped well with all demanded of them. The strike of 1903 mentioned earlier had some other effects on top of Inchicore's inability to fulfil current locomotive construction needs. One such effect was the provision of replacement boilers for the class '101' upgrade programme. The eight needed to fulfil the needs of this programme were ordered from the Vulcan Foundry and speedily delivered.

However, it is worth pointing out the underlying reason for this boiler upgrade. Freight train weights were now, on average, considerably heavier than previously and, with wet rails, the class '101' were prone to slipping which, when combined with the high demand for steam, caused losses in time. Coey accordingly ordered that a larger boiler be designed for the '101' to alleviate this shortage of steam and add about three tons adhesive weight. The

The Coey class '355' started as an 0-6-0 in 1903, but soon had to be modified as a 2-6-0. This drawing shows the original design.   *The Locomotive*

plan was progressively to reboiler the entire class as the smaller, older, boilers wore out. Eventually, the majority of the fleet were so rebuilt, and their lives extended well into the first half of the 20th century.

By this time it was apparent that this 1867 design had reached the limit of growth permitted by the 12 tons axle loading. With some of the branch lines now coming up to the 16 tons axle loading standard, Coey found he could enlarge both boiler and firebox. Away went the old oven type double smokebox doors, replaced by a conventional dished version. The resulting larger, heavier locomotives that ensued formed class '351', of which four were outshopped at the end of 1902. The boiler was interchangeable with the class '301' 4-4-0 in the interest of standardisation.

The traffic department was now pressing for increased weight goods trains as business picked up, and so Coey ordered the drawing office to prepare plans for an even larger and more powerful 0-6-0. At this time, Inchicore was still suffering from the effects of the strike which had led to the order on Neilson, Reid for the class '310' 4-4-0. So the new goods locomotive was eventually ordered from Messrs Sharp, Stewart & Co., Glasgow. The strike, while it lasted, had a marked effect on the procurement policy of the GS&WR in that shortly after it started, the Board decided to get tenders from the USA as well as the UK. The Great Northern and the Midland railways at that time had a few examples of Baldwin locomotives in service and Ivatt was contacted for his opinion on the suitability of that manufacturer. Before committing themselves the Locomotive Committee decided to postpone any decision on American engines 'until the Locomotive Engineer visits America and reports'. This decision resulted in Coey's trip to America in 1903; although no locomotive orders were ever placed there, he did come back with new ideas on boiler design, namely taper boilers, as we have seen in the previous chapter. Listed as class '355', the seven 0-6-0 locomotives were delivered speedily from Sharp, Stewart & Co. at the end of 1903. They were a completely new design having 19 inch by 26 inch cylinders and the largest boiler on the railway up to that time, with a heating surface of 1,535 sq. ft, nearly 200 sq. ft more than that of class '351'. It had also been intended to order a further two to the same specification from either Baldwins or the American Locomotive Company. However, the realisation that, no matter what the specification, they would have been completely non-standard brought about a change of mind for the Board. The economics of providing support for yet another class meant that the order was never placed. It remained for Coras Iompair Eireann (CIE), in later years, to arrange the supply of locomotives from America, when firmly in the diesel age.

With Robert away in America for some weeks, Maunsell stepped up temporarily and Inchicore, under his expert guidance, started to return to normality following the damaging strike. The chance to be in overall control gave him a clear feeling of the ultimate goal of succeeding Coey which was, eventually, to come his way.

The introduction of the class '355' enabled goods trains of 700 tons or more to be hauled, but the civil engineers were most unhappy about the 17 ton 11 cwt loading of the front axle. Some attempt at lightening this involved replacing the steel front buffer beam by one made of oak. However, the real culprit was the cylinder casting and motion plate which placed too much weight on the leading wheels. Coey was disappointed, and whether or not the cause lay with Sharp,

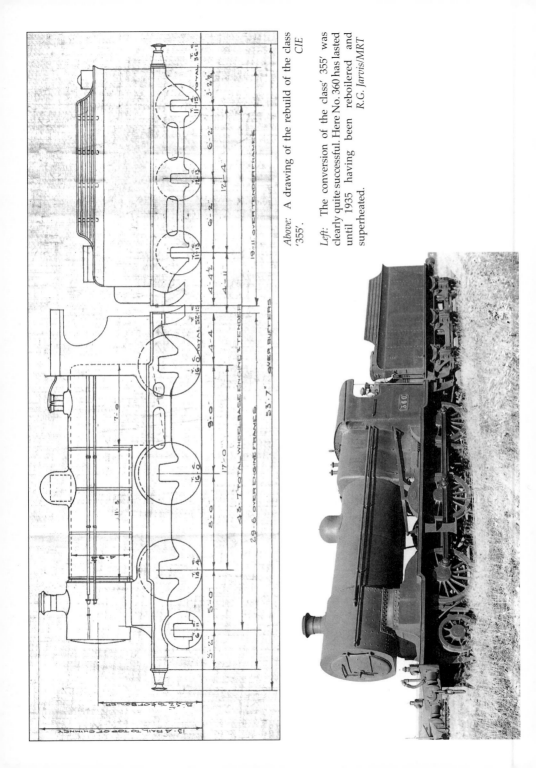

Above: A drawing of the rebuild of the class '355'.

CIE

Left: The conversion of the class' 355' was clearly quite successful. Here No. 360 has lasted until 1935 having been reboilered and superheated.

R.G. Jarvis/MRT

Stewart or Inchicore in failing to assess the front end weight is not clear to date. However, the remedy suggested by Robert was to rebuild the whole class as 2-6-0s, by extending the frames forward to accommodate front carrying wheels on a radial axle which was accomplished in 1907. In this guise they were acceptable and lived on until the late 1950s. In selecting the Mogul answer to this problem, Coey might well have been influenced by Maunsell, who had seen early examples of this type in service on the Indian Midland Railway as far back as 1893.

As some more powerful goods engines were needed, and mindful of the problems caused by the class '355' episode, Coey turned his thoughts to a 4-6-0, the first such arrangement to appear on the standard gauge in Ireland. The resulting class '362' was not a very successful design. The boiler was a lengthened version of that built for the '355s', some 14 ft 9¾ in. long, having the front tube plate recessed some 15 inches into the front ring. The smokebox was also a departure from Inchicore tradition in that it was the same diameter as the boiler outer plates. The six members of the class were built in two batches of three in 1905 and 1907.

On class '362' the running plate was raised over the coupled wheels with only one curve compared to the previous double curve of the class '355'. It was the first design to carry such a shape, which was to become a standard feature in styling at Inchicore on the rebuilds of the Coey 4-4-0s in later years. It also was adopted by Maunsell on the GS&WR, SE&CR and Southern Railway, and it has been speculated that Maunsell actually encouraged its adoption with his dictum of making things 'get-at-able', which in respect of access to coupling rod bosses and wheel bearings it certainly assisted no end.

A feature of these 4-6-0s was the employment of the class '355' cylinders, coupled axles and wheels, axleboxes, eccentrics, eccentric rods and rocking shafts. The longer front end meant that the piston rods had to be extended by some 3 ft 10 in. to meet with the connecting rods that drove onto the centre set of coupled wheels. This broke with tradition in that convention, up to then, had dictated that the drive was normally taken on the front axle for inside-cylinder types of this configuration. The use of class '355' wheels and motion by Coey was an attempt to economise on cost. The forward extension of the cylinders on the same slope as that of the class '355' necessitated raising the boiler centreline considerably to prevent them encroaching on the smokebox bottom. The slide bars were not connected to the cylinder casting, being supported by the motion plate and a supplementary plate across the frames. As with the '355s', the slide valves were placed on top of the cylinders, giving a very direct exhaust, but involving a rocking shaft to transmit the motion from the Stephenson eccentrics. Such a location for this type of valve had been used previously by Coey - on the compound 4-4-0 conversion and the class '355'. One other notable example of this valve layout was found on the Aspinall 4-4-2 on the L&YR.

The steeply inclined cylinders and valve chests caused an early modification to the class, in that they encroached into the base of the smokebox and caused ash and cinders to collect at the back and block the lower tubes. The smokebox was extended forward to give more volume and thus reduce the depth of ash collection. The second batch of three incorporated this modification from the start.

The '362s' were notable in that all six examples disappeared from the stock list by the early 1930s. What little can be gleaned from the very limited information

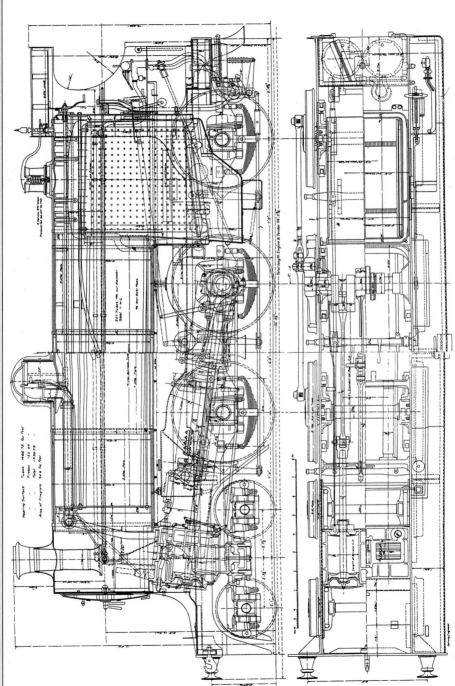

The Coey 4-6-0 as illustrated in the *Railway Engineer* for March 1906. The long extension of the piston rod is evident in this drawing.

Coey's 0-6-0, class '351', an improvement of the '101' class. No. 252 on a ballast train passes through Attanagh in 1958. *Drew Donaldson/Courtesy of Bill Scott*

The second batch of 4-6-0s had an extended smokebox. No. 366 of that batch is found at Cork. *National Railway Museum*

Table Four

The Goods Locomotives in Coey's Time

Designer	McDonnell	Coey	Coey	Coey	Coey
Class	101	351	355†	362	368
Arrangement	0-6-0	0-6-0	0-6-0	4-6-0	2-6-0
First batch built	1867	1903	1903	1905	1909
Number constructed	111*	8	7	6	4
Cyls (dia. and stroke)	18 in. x 24 in.	18 in. x 26 in.	19 in. x 26 in.	19 in. x 26 in.	19 in. x 26 in.
Coupled wheels	5 ft 1¾ in.	5 ft 1¾ in.	5 ft 1¾ in.	5 ft 1¾ in.	5 ft 1¾ in.
Bogie/leading wheels	n/a	n/a	n/a	3 ft 0 in.	3 ft 0 in.
Coupled wheelbase	15 ft 6 in.	16 ft 1 in.	17 ft 0 in.	14 ft 6 in.	16 ft 0 in.
Total wheelbase (engine)	15 ft 6 in.	16 ft 1 in.	17 ft 0 in.	24ft 10¾ in.	21 ft 9 in.
Boiler barrel length	9 ft 10 in.	10 ft 3¾ in.	11 ft 3 in.	14 ft 9¾ in.	11 ft 3 in.
Boiler dia. (inside)	4 ft 0 in.	4 ft 5¾ in.	4 ft 9¼ in.	4 ft 9½ in.	4 ft 10½ in.
Firebox length	5 ft 1 in.	5 ft 10 in.	7 ft 0 in.	7 ft 0 in.	7 ft 0 in.
Grate area	17.5 ft^2	20.4 ft^2	24.8 ft^2	24.8 ft^2	24.8 ft^2
Heating surface, firebox	96 ft^2	118 ft^2	132 ft^2	133 ft^2	138.5 ft^2
" " , tubes	764 ft	1,129 ft	1,403 ft	1,466.7 ft	1,446.5 ft
" " , TOTAL	860 ft	1,247 ft	1,535 ft	1,599.7 ft	1,585 ft
Weight, bogie/leading	n/a	n/a	n/a	12 t 18 cwt	7 t 13 cwt
" , leading	12 t 2 cwt	15 t 2 cwt	17 t 11 cwt	14 t 9 cwt	14 t 10 cwt
" , driving coupled	11 t 16 cwt	15 t 12 cwt	17 t 3 cwt	15 t 11 cwt	15 t 11 cwt
" , trailing	9 t 10 cwt	13 t 2 cwt	14 t 9 cwt	14 t 2 cwt	15 t 7 cwt
" , TOTAL	33 t 8 cwt	43 t 16 cwt	49 t 3 cwt	57 t 0 cwt	53 t 1 cwt
Boiler pressure	160 psi	160 psi	160 psi	160psi	160 psi
Tractive effort	17,130 lb.	18,550 lb.	20,760 lb.	21,220 lb.	20,760 lb.

* 64 of these built in batches as follows in Coey's time:

1881	1882	1885	1888	1889	1891	1896	1898	1899	1902	1903
6	12	4	4	4	4	2	4	4	4	8

† Later rebuilt as 2-6-0 to alleviate route limitation due to excessive axle loading.

A relatively unknown 0-6-0 of Coey was that rebuilt from two of the four 0-6-2Ts. Here No. 212, one of that pair rests at Waterford between trips. Although of good tractive effort, this example acquired the nickname 'The Reverend Mother' due to its slow and stately acceleration on full regulator.

Drew Donaldson/Courtesy of Bill Scott

Table Five

McDonnell Tank Designs

Class	47	201	203
Type	0-4-4	0-6-4	0-6-4
First batch built	1879	1876	1879
Number constructed	35*	2	4
Cyls (dia. and stroke)	16 in. x 20 in.	18 in. x 24 in.	18 in. x 24 in.
Coupled wheels	5 ft 8½ in.	4 ft 6½ in.	4 ft 6½ in.
Leading/bogie wheels	n/a	n/a	n/a
Trailing radial/bogie wheels	3 ft 9 in.	3 ft 8½ in.	3 ft 9 in.
Coupled wheelbase	6 ft 0 in.	13 ft 3 in.	15 ft 6 in.
Total wheelbase (engine)	22 ft 4½ in.	24 ft 9½ in.	25 ft 9½ in.
Boiler barrel length	9 ft 9¾ in.	9 ft 4 in.	9 ft 9 in.
Boiler dia. (inside)	3 ft 7¾ in.	4 ft 3 in.	4 ft 3 in.
Grate area	15.25 ft²	18.8 ft²	18.8 ft²
Heating surface, firebox	78.5 ft²	84.5 ft²	103.5 ft²
" " , tubes	677.0ft²	900.0 ft²	900.0 ft²
" " , TOTAL	755.5 ft²	984.5 ft²	1,003.5 ft²
Tank capacity (gallons)	1,044	1,320	1,130
Weight, bogie/leading	n/a	n/a	n/a
" , leading coupled	11 t 14 cwt	11 t 18 cwt	12 t 13 cwt
" , driving	11 t 14 cwt	11 t 4 cwt	11 t 8 cwt
" , trailing coupled	n/a	11 t 6 cwt	11 t 12cwt
" , trailing radial/bogie	17 t 14 cwt	12 t 8 cwt	15 t 13 cwt
" , TOTAL	44 t 12 cwt	46 t 16 cwt	51 t 6 cwt
Boiler pressure	160 psi	140 psi	150 psi
Tractive effort	10,165lb.	16,980 lb.	18,190 lb.

Note: *20 built by Aspinall from 1883 onwards.

Table Six

Ivatt Tank Designs

Class	207	42	35
Type	0-6-0	2-4-2	4-4-2
First batch built	1887	1893	1894
Number constructed	4	6	6*
Cyls (dia. & stroke)	18 in. x 24 in.	16 in. x 20 in.	16 in. x 20 in.
Coupled wheels	4 ft 6½ in.	5 ft 8½ in.	5 ft 8½ in.
Leading/bogie wheels	n/a	3 ft 9 in.	3 ft 0 in.
Trailing radial wheels	n/a	3 ft 9 in.	3 ft 9 in.
Coupled wheelbase	15 ft 6 in.	7 ft 11 in.	7 ft 11 in.
Total wheelbase (engine)	15 ft 6 in.	19 ft 11 in.	24 ft 8¾ in.
Boiler barrel length	9 ft 9¾ in.	9 ft 4 in.	9 ft 4 in.
Boiler dia. (inside)	4 ft 3 in.	3 ft 9¾ in.	3 ft 9¾ in.
Grate area	18.8 ft²	16.0 ft²	16.0 ft²
Heating surface, firebox	112.5 ft²	83.8 ft²	83.8 ft²
" " , tubes	938.0 ft²	770.0 ft²	770.0 ft²
" " , TOTAL	1050.5 ft²	853.8 ft²	853.8 ft²
Tank capacity (gallons)	945	1,250	1,130
Weight, bogie/leading	n/a	11 t 12 cwt	11 t 0 cwt
" , leading coupled	12 t 10 cwt	n/a	n/a
" , driving	15 t 16 cwt	12 t 10 cwt	12 t 10 cwt
" , trailing coupled	16 t 6 cwt	11 t 16 cwt	12 t 10 cwt
" , trailing radial	n/a	10 t 14 cwt	12 t 10 cwt
" , TOTAL	44 t 12 cwt	46 t 2 cwt	48 t 10 cwt
Boiler pressure	150 psi	160 psi	160 psi
Tractive effort	18,190lb.	10,165 lb.	10,165 lb.

Note: *Two built under Ivatt, (converted from 2-4-2's). Remainder under Coey (1901).

regarding them is that they were relatively poor engines with considerable problems associated with rough riding combined with a low axle loading of the leading drivers. Derailments were all too frequent. Coey had obviously failed to provide a satisfactory answer to the need for additional powerful goods locomotives. One feature which certainly worked against the class was its total wheelbase of 47 ft 6 in., which would have been too great for the moderately sized turntables on the railway, many of which were only 45 ft in diameter.

By 1908, more goods locomotives were needed and Coey, having realised that the rebuilt class '355' was just as, if not more, capable than the class '362', and certainly more reliable, decided to produce more based on the former design in its 2-6-0 guise. The major changes in the class '368' that emerged were a reduction in the coupled wheelbase of 9 inches achieved by bringing the leading wheels back by that amount, and the introduction of a Belpaire firebox, the first time that this latter feature was employed at Inchicore. The resulting engine had substantially the same tractive effort as for the class '362' 4-6-0 and proved very successful. Four were outshopped in 1909. The employment of the Belpaire box was so beneficial that the earlier class '333s' were rebuilt with them later, as were many of the other 4-4-0s.

At this stage, further goods locomotive developments under Coey came to a halt. His health problems were growing, and the pace of develoment slackened.

With the successful trials of superheating on the class '321' 4-4-0 it was only a matter of time before this was to be applied to the goods locomotives. One of the final design tasks ordered by Robert Coey was to build a further batch of four class '351', two of which were fitted with the Phoenix type superheaters. This cannot have made the engines look very nice, with the extended smokebox and the chimney right in front that this form of superheater entailed. As a result the installation was removed after a relatively short time in service. The application of superheating continued, and Maunsell took an active interest in what was going on. A further batch of class '351s' was planned incorporating the Schmidt design of superheater, but Coey was not to see these into service. They appeared under Maunsell's name in 1913, and proved immediately successful with their tractive effort of 24,320 lb., the greatest of all GS&WR locomotives at that time.

To round off the goods engine story, there must be included the tale of the two 0-6-2 tanks converted to 0-6-0 tender types in 1910. In many respects they were very similar to the class '351' except for the coupled wheels which were 4 ft 6½ in. as against the 5 ft 1¾ in. of that class. They proved useful engines and lived on for nearly 50 years after their conversion.

Whilst all these developments had been progressing, there was a small but important aspect involving tank engines, never very numerous on the GS&WR but nevertheless advantageous for certain duties.

The tank locomotive was never very prolific on the GS&WR scene and was mainly used on shunting and short range stopping passenger services. It was not until 1866 that the first examples, a small batch of saddle tanks, appeared, after the Cork and Youghal Railway was taken over.

The earliest Inchicore output of tank locomotives was for shunting, being rebuilds by McDonnell of old Wakefield goods engines, the exact types involved being lost in the mists of history, but probably 0-6-0s or 0-4-2s.

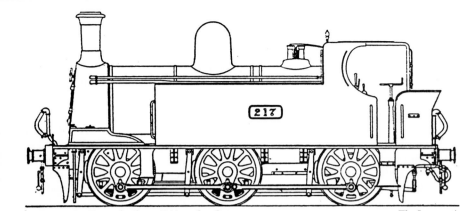

This Ivatt 0-6-0T was built in 1901 under Coey. *The Locomotive*

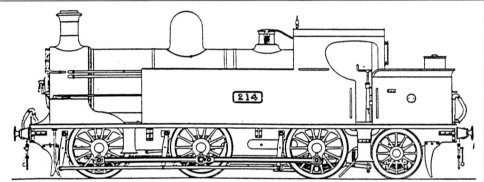

The Coey 0-6-2T of 1903. Built for duties on the Drumcondra link, two of the four were converted to 0-6-0 tender types in 1910. *The Locomotive*

The modified McDonnell 0-6-4T used for departmental duties from 1897. *The Locomotive*

McDonnell himself only produced two designs of tanks, of 0-4-4T and 0-6-4T arrangement, as part of his standardisation programme. The latter were the first of their type in the British Isles. The 0-4-4Ts are the ones mentioned in Chapter Two, starting life as Fairlies, and were to be increased by a further 20 engines built under Aspinall. It appears that the large spacing between the coupled wheels and rear bogie was the result of the original Fairlie layout, and was a distinguishing feature of these locomotives.

The 0-6-4Ts of classes '201' and '203' had many features in common with the class '101' Standard Goods, mainly the motion, and were almost exclusively used on shunting duties. It appears surprising that such a lengthy design should be produced for shunting in the close confines and tight curves associated with goods yards.

Ivatt had been responsible for the introduction of small batches of tanks of the 0-6-0, 2-4-2 and 4-4-2 arrangements, the latter two specifically for passenger work.

Robert Coey thus had a small range of, in some cases somewhat dated, tank designs to hand in 1896. His first move was to withdraw the McDonnell class '201' pair of 0-6-4 tanks and relegate them to departmental stock duties. His first foray into the supply of tank locomotives was to design some minor modifications, prior to further production, to the Ivatt 4-4-2T of 1894, the two of which then at work proving useful and reliable engines. Two variants were built under Coey, four of class '27' and four of class '37'. The latter were to all intents and purposes identical to the Ivatt design, save for a small modification to the tank. These two batches were outshopped in 1900 (class '27') and 1901 (class '37').

Much of the work for these new tanks was branch line passenger use in the southern areas of the GS&WR, where they superseded the older types then in use. The recent absorption of some smaller railways in this part of Ireland produced the need for new, more modern, tanks of a standard design to replace the various inherited antiquities.

Also in 1901, Coey produced a new variant of the Ivatt 0-6-0T which employed the boiler developed for the final batches of the class '101', then coming to the end of its long production and development cycle, the final numbers of which were turned out in 1902 and 1903.

The relatively minor changes wrought by Coey to the Ivatt designs meant that the only true new Coey tank locomotive was the 0-6-2T of 1903. As with the class '310' 4-4-0 and class '355' 0-6-0, the four engines constructed had to be ordered from outside. By the time the order was placed, Neilson, Reid & Co. and Sharp, Stewart & Co. had merged with Dübs to form the North British Locomotive Company, and it was this new conglomerate which supplied the locomotives. Delivery was commendably quick and the engines were placed on the Drumcondra link line service. However, the weight bug had struck again, and the 58 tons of these locomotives proved too much for this newly constructed line and drew some complaints from the Civil Engineering Department. Recourse to running with the side tanks only partially filled resulted in limited range and reduced usefulness of the class. Accordingly, two of them were soon withdrawn from service and converted to 0-6-0 tender types as mentioned earlier, in which guise they served until the 1950s, as indeed did the two remaining tanks. Of the two conversions, No. 212 was based at

Waterford for many years, where it eventually acquired the nick-name 'The Reverend Mother' owing to its propensity to accelerate slowly only to a moderate speed no matter how wide or fast the regulator was opened.

Matters such as the apparently inadequate weight control when resorting to outside contractors ruffled Coey's pride in the excellence normally associated with Inchicore products. No further resort to outside builders was to be made under him, and indeed, not until the early 1920s did the GS&WR have any engines built elsewhere. This was only occasioned by events stemming from the creation of the Irish Free State and the associated Civil War situation.

Coey designed no further tank locomotives and it was left to Maunsell's successor, Edward Watson, to bring out the next new tank design. Maunsell, when he took over from Robert, did indulge in some schemes for large tank engines, but his move to Ashford in 1913 stemmed any meaningful developments. His only tank design which got built, the single 0-4-2ST works shunter, was a pure hybrid, made up almost exclusively of standard parts.

Table Seven

Coey Tank Designs

Class	27	217	211
Type	4-4-2T	0-6-0T	0-6-2T
First batch built	1900	1901	1903
Number constructed	4	4	4*
Cyls (dia. and stroke)	17 in. x 22 in.	18 in. x 24 in.	18 in. x 26 in.
Coupled wheels	5 ft 8½ in.	4 ft 6½ in.	4 ft 6½ in.
Leading/bogie wheels	3 ft 0 in.	n/a	n/a
Trailing radial wheels	3 ft 9 in.	n/a	3 ft 9 in.
Coupled wheelbase	7 ft 9 in.	15 ft 6 in.	16 ft 1 in.
Total wheelbase (engine)	25 ft 5¼ in.	15 ft 6 in.	22 ft 1 in.
Boiler barrel length	9 ft 7 in.	9 ft 10 in.	10 ft 3 in.
Boiler dia. (inside)	4 ft 0 in.	4 ft 3in.	4 ft 5 in.
Grate area	17.5 ft^2	19.3 ft^2	20.4 ft^2
Heating surface, firebox	97.1 ft^2	105.0 ft^2	118.0 ft^2
" " , tubes	753.9 ft^2	934.0 ft^2	1,129.0 ft^2
" " , TOTAL	851.0 ft^2	1,039.0 ft^2	1,147.0 ft^2
Tank capacity (gallons)	1,425	730	1,050
Weight, bogie/leading	12 t 14 cwt	n/a	n/a
" , leading coupled	n/a	13 t 0 cwt	15 t 6 cwt
" , driving	15 t 0 cwt	12 t 10 cwt	17 t 3 cwt
" , trailing coupled	15 t 2 cwt	15 t 6 cwt	14 t 18 cwt
" , trailing radial	11 t 4 cwt	n/a	10 t 13 cwt
" , TOTAL	54 t 0 cwt	43 t 16 cwt	58 t 0 cwt
Boiler pressure	160 psi	160 psi	160 psi
Tractive effort	12,620 lb.	19,400 lb.	21,020 lb.

*Built by North British Locomotive Co. Two later converted to 0-6-0 tender.

Chapter Seven

Carriages, Wagons and Retirement: 1880-1921

Thirteen years after the installation of Alexander McDonnell, the carriage and wagon stock came under his charge, as witness his revised title of Locomotive, Carriage and Wagon Superintendent. Prior to this there had been a separate position responsible for rolling stock, held by one Harry Corlett, who retired in 1877.

Shortly after this date McDonnell ordered a set of new designs of carriages to be set out with the aim of replacing much of the by then outdated stock of early carriages, most of it six-wheeled. These new designs were also six-wheeled with a length of 30 ft, the first class having four compartments, seconds five and thirds six. These designs became the standard for the following 20 years, being supplemented by Aspinall, Ivatt and Coey. Many of these coaches lasted through into the 1950s, being used on branch lines and for excursion trains.

As with many of the railways across the Irish Sea, none of the earlier versions of six-wheeled stock had lavatories provided. Train travel was still unhurried, with lengthy stops *en route* on the longer runs, permitting passengers to take advantage of the station facilities. Life was still sufficiently relaxed to permit this. However, in 1882, the first lavatory-equipped coaches appeared in the form of first/second composites, yet on these early versions only the first class passengers had access to the lavatory accommodation.

Bogie coaches made their first appearance in 1885, in the form of a single trial example, with a small batch of production models following in 1888. Robert Coey would have been heavily involved in setting up this production run in the modernised carriage and wagon shops, the old carriage shop at the eastern end of the works having been enlarged and converted into the paint shop some short time previously. This old carriage shop had been approached by small turntables, totally inadequate for bogie stock, which itself needed more production space. However, it was not until Coey took office in 1896 that the decision to manufacture more bogie stock was made. Six-wheeled stock continued to be built. The one major change to carriages which appeared was under Ivatt in 1892, when gas lighting replaced the old oil lighting in production vehicles.

In 1898 the take-over of the Waterford and Wexford Railway brought the important ferry port of Rosslare into the GS&WR. Boat trains to and from that port were initiated from Cork and Dublin for which new bogie stock was built. The 66 ft coaches were the largest built at Inchicore during Coey's time there. Rosslare increased in popularity as a port of entry due to these direct rail connections with other parts of Ireland.

Dining cars were first introduced in 1898 for the Day Mail expresses to and from Queenstown (Cobh) in the form of two 3-car sets consisting of a first class saloon and a second class coach, both with centre corridors, which were coupled to a first class dining car with kitchen. The second class coach was arranged as a dining compartment over about half its length, this end being that coupled to the kitchen. All were 45 ft long. Initially they had no connection to the rest of the train, but in about 1900 gangways were added at the outer ends. Also appearing in 1900 was the first third class dining car, built specially for the 6.00 am Cork-Dublin mail express.

As 1901 approached, the GS&WR took stock of the carriages acquired in its take-over of adjacent railways, these being the Waterford-Dungaven, Lismore and Waterford and Central Ireland Railways. The carriages of those lines were mainly obsolescent four- and six-wheelers in a dilapidated and worn out condition and were immediately withdrawn, being temporarily replaced with GS&WR stock. This precipitated an acute stock shortage and the carriage department at Inchicore was very busy over the next few years as Coey ordered new vehicles. When it was obvious that the GS&WR could not supply enough in time, orders were placed with English suppliers to make up the shortfall. Around this time the length of new stock was set at 50 ft.

Electric lighting, Coey ordered, was to become standard as from 1903 and considerable investment was made to satisfy this directive. However, as time went by, the maintenance costs of this new form of lighting rose to a point where the Board ordered the reversion to gas lighting, despite the obvious hazards if an accident took place. It was not until 1915 that electric lighting returned as a standard, although some coaches obviously escaped this as examples employing gas lighting were still to be seen in service as late as the 1950s. The directive ordering this change stemmed from the publicity given to the dangers of gas lighting brought about by the accidents in 1910 at Hawes Junction (12 killed) and 1913 Ais Gill (14 killed) on the Midland Railway. Both involved fires spreading rapidly through the wreckage, caused by damaged gas tanks.

In 1903 a special order was placed with the carriage department for a state carriage for the GS&WR portion of the tour of Ireland by King Edward VII in late July of that year. Fifty feet in length, this vehicle had a custom-built body incorporating a smoking room, reception room and Queen's room, the elaborate decor of these being provided by the Dublin firm of Sibthorpe. It has been described as the finest piece of coaching stock ever produced by Inchicore. This vehicle still exists, and has been restored to its former glory in which it is hoped to be used by the Irish President and visiting dignitaries. Other Irish railways also produced some special carriages for this Royal occasion, notably the Midland Great Western Railway (MGWR), which turned out a sumptuous vehicle with an observation end to permit the Royal party to view the scenery from the comfortable armchairs provided. This particular vehicle, originally on four-wheeled bogies, eventually came to Inchicore on the formation of the Great Southern Railway (GSR) in the mid-1920s, by which time it had been rebuilt on six-wheeled bogies. This coach survived until the 1950s, one of its last recorded uses being to form the final vehicle in the special train provided for the Papal Envoy's visit to Ireland in the mid-1950s.

A brief foray into the then fashionable railmotor scene was made in 1904, when Coey introduced the first, and only, such vehicle on the GS&WR. Railmotors were all the rage in England then, and Inchicore followed the lead with this design. It was put into service on the Cashel branch before a series of trials on the Drumcondra link. It was not particularly successful, the small vertical-boilered engine barely producing enough power to propel the core vehicle at a respectable speed and was withdrawn by Maunsell in 1912. The body shell was converted into a tri-composite brake coach which itself was scrapped by Watson in 1914. So ended the experiment into railmotor use. Coey was not too much dismayed by this failure, as many other railways in the British Isles were finding the same problem and phasing out such stock, their traffic departments having attempted to increase their utility by expecting them to haul extra vans on occasions, a task which quickly wore them out.

Side corridor coaches appeared in 1907, 52 ft in length, with eight compartments typical of the third class version. Matters so far as Robert Coey was concerned, ceased here, for no more significant carriage developments were to be made until Edward Watson increased the standard length to 57 ft upon his taking office in 1914.

That mundane stock, goods wagons, totalled over 3,500 examples of all types when Coey took office as Works Manager. Many were very dated in their layout, and one was to find such antiquities as vans with sliding roofs in service for many years after this. As goods traffic increased, largely consisting of coal, farm produce and cattle movements, new, more robust and heavier stock was produced. Freight traffic in Ireland never achieved the levels reached in England, largely due to the lack of large manufacturing concerns. The economy mainly revolved around agriculture with its seasonal variations. However, many hundreds of replacement and extra goods vehicles were produced under Robert Coey from the wagon shops at Inchicore.

Towards the end of the first decade of the 20th century, Coey and Maunsell planned an update to the works. Up to now, steam or gas engines were prevalent for driving machinery, electricity only being introduced in a small measure. The major change decided by Robert and Richard was the construction of a power house containing two 300 hp Sulzer diesel-driven generator sets to supply the current, thus bringing the works fully into the 20th century. The workforce now totalled some 1,700 in all capacities. The design side was, at all times, minimal, with only four senior and five junior draughtsmen under the competent guidance of Ernest Joynt, the chief draughtsman.

With the increased call for carriage and goods stock servicing and construction, Robert was deeply involved in planning some major alterations to Inchicore, which now covered some 87 acres in extent. The size to which the GS&WR had grown demanded a considerable increase in manufacturing capacity. Stock levels had now increased to 283 locomotives, 885 passenger coaches plus 7,852 goods vehicles, and the throughput in servicing and repairs was outstripping capacity. Richard Maunsell, a past master of organisation, in his capacity of Works Manager took much of the responsibility on his shoulders, thus easing the load on Robert considerably in his time of ill-health.

The major changes at Inchicore to cope with the increased capacity involved the closing of the old carriage and wagon shop for conversion to a new running shed, the previous running shed of Sancton Woods being turned into a carriage shed. New facilities included some new and extensive carriage and wagon

GS&WR brake third No. 863 of 1906.   *John Alsop Collection*

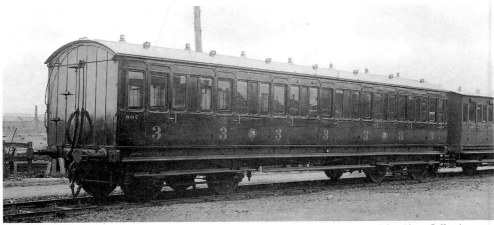

GS&WR carriage No. 807.   *John Alsop Collection*

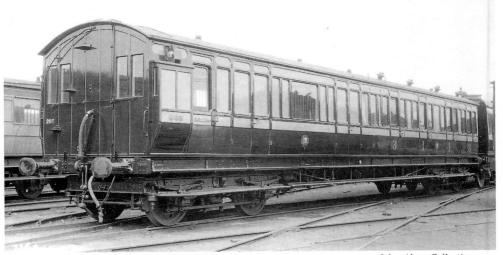

GS&WR brake composite No. 865 of 1907.   *John Alsop Collection*

shops for both new manufacture and repairs and the powerhouse mentioned above.

The pressures on Robert were immense during this works' reorganisation. He placed much reliance on Richard Maunsell for overseeing the many changes being made, their close working relationship being of great benefit. Maunsell showed complete capability in taking on much of the responsibility and ensuring the smooth implementation of the new developments. The years associated with his smooth running of Inchicore works before the onset of Coey's illness brought Maunsell's expertise to the notice of railway authorities elsewhere. There was an attempt to arrange a position for him as Works Manager on the Great Northern Railway at Doncaster under Ivatt, but this was thwarted by the then Chairman of that railway, who stipulated that one F. Wintour was to be given the job. Maunsell was to remain at Inchicore for some years more, but events across the water were eventually to result in his departure for Ashford and the SE&CR.

Robert was not to see the completion of these alterations, for they were only finished in 1913, two years after he left the scene. It remained for Richard Maunsell to be the first beneficiary of the updating and expansion.

In the closing years of Robert's superintendency, his wife Elizabeth and their daughter Maud often boarded the Cork expresses at Kingsbridge to visit Robert's sister Mary in that city. Mary's husband, Robert Parkhill, was an established businessman there, being a Director of wholesalers Messrs Dwyer and Co. as well as the Southern Metropole Hotels Ltd, in addition to being a pillar of the Methodist church in Cork. The house in which the Parkhills lived, Beaumont House, Douglas, stood in extensive grounds with stables for the horses. Maud enjoyed the company of her cousins, Edith, Ivie and Lilian, during these visits and she recounted with delight the happy times she spent around the grounds of this spacious property. Pressures of work in Dublin prevented Robert from making this trip on other than the odd occasion, but when he did, his deputy Maunsell was at hand to continue overseeing Inchicore progress.

As the years progressed, and 1911 approached, Robert continued to involve himself deeply in the Inchicore output, with increasing breaks due to his failing health. Never a very communicative man outside his family circles, he kept many problems to himself, only delegating out that which he felt could be safely handled by his subordinates. His personal relationship with the capable Richard Maunsell was close enough to enable him to confide some of his worries. Maunsell was well thought of in the works, much respected by all, and often involved in the design phase of new locomotive developments. Certainly if his future design episodes are to be considered he gained much valuable experience working with Coey. Joynt relates that the teamwork of Coey and Maunsell was such that the whole atmosphere of the works made it a pleasant place in which to be employed.

The close working relationship was becoming more evident on the design side as styling changes appeared on the new types under construction as we have seen earlier. These features became more apparent after Maunsell had left Dublin for Ashford in the eventual layout of many of his locomotives built for the SE&CR and the Southern Railway. The one feature, mentioned earlier, which shows a clear link is the layout of running plate shape over the coupled wheels of the single Maunsell 4-4-0 built at Inchicore shortly after Robert retired, and the 'D1', 'E1' and 'L1' 4-4-0s of the two English railways. The new running plate shape adopted for Coey's 4-6-0 and 2-6-0 showed the first signs of what was to become a Maunsell trait, so the railways in England have a Coey legacy in that context. Even if it was Maunsell that suggested this type of running plate, it must have been approved and adopted by Coey as a practical improvement.

But the habit of bottling things up obviously had an effect on Robert, as he was now beginning to be quite badly affected by stress and migraine attacks. In early 1911, he decided to consider retiring. He was approaching 60, and being rather well off by that time, saw no reason to defer his departure. The Board were accordingly informed as to his intention, and Maunsell suggested as a capable replacement. The Board meeting of 30th June, 1911 therefore minuted that upon the retirement of Coey the Locomotive Superintendent's position would be filled by Richard Maunsell, so keeping up the long-standing Inchicore tradition of passing on the job that way.

One of the final matters which would have come Robert's way was the 1911 locomotive exchange with the Great Northern Railway of Ireland (GNR (I)). This was to see if there were any material differences in locomotive performance of that railway and the GS&WR so far as the express types were concerned. The types chosen for this exercise were all 4-4-0s, the GNR (I) supplying class Nos. 136 and 113, with class '305' No. 307 and class '321' No. 322 provided by the GS&WR. Such data as has survived indicated little difference in coal consumption, 39.4 lb. per mile for the GS&WR types as against 39.6 lb. per mile for the GNR (I). The limited evidence unearthed points towards a somewhat cavalier approach by the crews involved. The GS&WR fireman, Cummins, originally engaged was removed at some stage after what appears to be adverse comment on his firing techniques. The GNR (I) fireman, Wallace, on the GS&WR had an accident with a coal pick on an up train from Cork and had to be replaced. In addition to all this the Northern crew were rather fond of their drink and a fracas arose in a Cork pub one evening, resulting in them getting the worst of the affair.

The five week exercise failed to have a lasting effect upon locomotive development North or South. The only real conclusion one can draw from such evidence as is available being that North/South relationships then, as now, were sometimes strained. Coey was in the process of preparing for retirement and probably the document resulting from this exercise was quietly filed into obscurity.

By this time, Maud had been installed in England, at Harrogate College, for nearly a year. The Head Mistress of that school was a Miss W.E. Jones from Belfast, who was a cousin of Robert Coey's wife Elizabeth: 'A really regal person' in Maud's own words. Prior to being sent to Harrogate Maud had been educated at home by a governess, whom she did not get on with at all: 'My English governess said I was so stupid she simply could not teach me! Charming, I simply hated her!'

The school was to prove very popular with Maud, so Robert had no hesitation in moving from Dublin to Yorkshire upon retirement, initially settling in Scarborough. The move and cessation of the daily worries obviously benefited him, as his health improved and the family spent the next few years happily established in Scarborough during term time and moving up to the Turnberry Hotel in Scotland for the holidays. Maud had shown a keen sporting streak at School and the Scottish holidays enabled her to receive extra coaching in golf, by far her most favourite sport.

In the early days of his retirement, Robert may well have reflected on the use of his locomotives on the Dublin-Cobh weekly service for the White Star and Cunard shipping lines. The ill-fated *Titanic* of the former, built in Belfast, made her first (and last) call at Cobh in April 1912, and some passengers would have been transferred from the train for that fateful voyage, whereas the sister ship *Olympic* served for many trouble-free years and would have taken on board many thousands who travelled to Cobh drawn by Robert's locomotives.

The loss of the *Titanic* touched the lives of many in and around Belfast, especially those who had been involved in her design and construction. Further afield, at Scarborough, the Coey's were saddened by this tragedy, as Robert had frequently heard reports of progress in the ship's construction from brothers James and Henry who had, from their York Road offices, watched the huge vessel rise in the nearby shipyard. In later years Elizabeth Coey was to find herself distantly related to the Andrews family who had suffered the loss of one member on the *Titanic*. Thomas Andrews, Managing Director of Harland and Wolff shipyard and who, it is said, had a large say in the final detail design of the vessel, stayed on board the sinking ship and was one of the 1,490 that perished out of the 2,201 on board.* Ulster life is such that in disasters of this magnitude someone, somewhere, will have a connection with those involved. Thomas Andrews had a sister and two brothers. It was the sister that provided the link to the Coey family, in that Elizabeth, Robert's wife, had a cousin Victoria Jones whose son, Thibeaudeau married the daughter of this sister. Victoria was, in fact, the sister of Miss W.E. Jones, Maud's headmistress at Harrogate College. The two other Andrews brothers, John and James, were to become famous in their own right, John becoming Prime Minister of Northern Ireland from 1940 to 1943, and James rising through the legal profession to become Lord Chief Justice of Northern Ireland.

Robert's mother, Sarah, was justly proud of her eldest son, who had risen to the top in a demanding profession. Despite advancing deafness which made her seem dour and withdrawn, she and James Coey bade a fond farewell to Robert at the end of a brief visit to them, still living at No. 5, The Glen at the top end of the Limestone Road, before he departed for England. Robert's brothers, James and Henry, still fully employed at the York Road offices of the NCC, and whom we shall meet in the second half of this book, were both living nearby, so the family in and around Belfast was still relatively intact. Age was creeping on for both Sarah and James Senior, and the comforting knowledge of sons and a daughter nearby must have given them peace of mind.

---

* Figures from the *Report on the Loss of the SS Titanic* (HMSO, 1912).

Anne Parkhill

Sarah and James Coey around 1905-10

The last home of Robert Coey's parents in Belfast. No 5, The Glen. *Author*

Ouchy, the lakeside suburb of Lausanne from where the Coeys would have departed on steamer
trips.   *Author's Collection*

Andermatt in 1924, a small but important town commanding a major route into the centre of the
country. The Aldershot of Switzerland.   *Author's Collection*

Chapter Eight

Travel and the Retirement Years: 1921-1934

With the gradual return of his health following his early retirement, Robert began to think about exploring Europe, always an ambition of his, but initially thwarted by World War I. The Coeys spent the war years in Scarborough, Robert happy enough to remain retired and most certainly pleased to be away from the troubles, which led up to the Easter Uprising in Dublin, then brewing in Ireland. Inchicore works was not so badly affected by this as it was later during the Civil War. Not until 1921 was he able to achieve his ambition of travel. The family accordingly left for Switzerland on 15th September, 1921, their destination being Lausanne. The journey, accomplished non-stop, took 32 hours from Harrogate to which they had moved at the end of the war. According to Robert's own account the crossing from Dover to Boulogne was on a calm moonlit night and the longest train journey, from Paris to Lausanne, took 10 hours. The portion from London to Dover, over the South Eastern & Chatham Railway could well have involved a locomotive designed by Richard Maunsell, now the CME of that line.

There was an ulterior motive to this trip, in that Maud showed a considerable aptitude for languages and the Coeys, being rather well off, wished their daughter to practice this as well as attending a finishing school there. Robert and Elizabeth took up residence at the Hotel Mont Fleure, about half a mile from the lakeside at Lausanne, whilst Maud went to live with a French widow just outside the town, where she had the company of a Dutch girl for a few months. 'They are all on the best of terms and as jolly as sandboys', as Robert wrote to his brother-in-law, the Revd James Parkhill, husband of Catherine Coey. Maud also attended the local lycée for literature and painting classes in the company of several other English girls whose parents had brought them out to Switzerland for their final education.

Lausanne was, most certainly, greatly appreciated by the Coeys, in that the atmosphere was clear, the town clean and well-ordered with public buildings which Robert clearly appreciated 'such as the Post Office, the Courts of Justice, etc. are magnificent buildings both as regards exterior decoration and internal accommodation and finish as also are the banks, of which there are half a dozen or more. I have not seen anything like them anywhere', he wrote. It was, by all accounts, an economic way of living. 'We pay 12s. a day each here and are doing it cheaper than living in England, although things have gone up in price here just as much as there . . .'

The weather also agreed with Robert and Elizabeth, and they were able to relax and soak up the ambience of a classic Swiss lakeside town. 'Ever since we came the sun has been shining out of a clear calm sky and beating down on us so that it is hotter by the lake than in among the trees'. They obviously travelled around the local area to get the feel of the land, taking note of the agricultural nature of the countryside: 'Of course the hill slopes are covered with vines and the peasants have a hard life in the fields, where beside grapes they grow all

A typical Swiss mountain railway of the 1920s. This example is the Rigi Railway near Lucerne.
(Both) Author's Collection

kinds of green stuff. Apples and pears are growing everywhere in the open fields by the roadside in great quantities . . .'

They stayed in Lausanne until late December, departing for Adelboden and the ski slopes just before Christmas. This was to please Maud, as her sporting accomplishments covered skiing and skating. It was a jolly time, as Maud had the company of a friend from Lausanne and Robert and Elizabeth entertained Maud's old headmistress from Harrogate College, Mina Jones, and her sister Lena. The Swiss winter scenery had a great effect on Robert and he waxed eloquent about this in his Christmas letter to James Parkhill:

> When we came there was no snow except a little on the high tops, but it has been snowing for the last two days and nights, and now everything is covered with about a foot of white, dry, glistening snow and today the sun is shining bright and warm out of a cloudless sky of dark blue. In the brilliant atmosphere of these altitudes it feels quite hot and yet the atmosphere is below freezing point. We are 4,500 feet above sea level and the mountains right in front of us, about ½ mile across, rise up another 3,000 to 4,500 feet all white and sparkling in the brilliant sunshine.

After a Christmas and New Year spent at Adelboden the family returned to Lausanne for six months to enable Maud to continue her studies. On 1st July, 1922 they left Lausanne and travelled around the Swiss resorts in the mountainous region, where they found large numbers of English tourists and, in the more fashionable places, considerable numbers of Americans also. One of the many places in their itinerary was Zermatt, where they spent part of August. Robert was certainly interested by the cog-wheel mountain railways, the majority in those days still steam powered. One such experience is described by him thus: 'It was all very interesting, especially the trip up to the "Gorner Grat" by cog wheel railway, to a height of over 10,000 feet, and where one is in the centre of a grand amphitheatre of snow clad peaks and glaciers glistening pure white in the brilliant sunshine for miles and miles around.'

Leaving Switzerland at the end of September, the Coeys then travelled to Italy where, after visiting Stresa, on the shores of Lake Maggiore, they spent time in Milan and Venice before settling into rooms at the Hotel Albion in Florence from the 1st November. Maud wished to add Italian to her many languages and, Florence being a centre of the art world, some drawing lessons as well. Whilst Robert's interest certainly ranged to architecture and art, there were some features of Florence which clearly annoyed him: 'The noise is abominable, it arises from motor horns of a peculiarly ear-splitting kind, the trams running through narrow streets within one foot of the footpath, the shouting and whistling of the boys, etc.'

There were, however, many aspects of Florence which Robert appreciated. He took an especial interest in the frescoes which were to be found in some of the old churches as well as the palaces dating from the 14th century. His ordered mind was taxed by the apparent lack of planning as regards the town layout: 'Our room looks right across the Arno to the most typical bit of Medieval house architectures I have yet seen, built right out of the river 70 or 80 feet high, without the slightest order or regularity, etc.'

The lakeside vineyards mentioned in Robert Coey's letters. Although this photograph was taken in 1954, the scene would have been very similar in 1923. Note the train on the lakeside line.
Author's Collection

These 2-Do-1 electric locomotives were entering service during the time Robert Coey and his family were living in Switzerland.   *Author's Collection*

Maud's Italian studies kept them in Florence until the end of March 1923, when they departed for a three week stay in Rome followed by a fortnight in Naples. Whilst in Rome a Mrs Rowell and her daughter Pat were with them as companions on their rambles around the city.

The weather for all those five weeks was good, especially Naples, where: '. . . the sunshine there was glorious, not a cloud in the clear blue sky from sunrise to sunset every day . . .' They took advantage of their time in Naples to pay a two day visit to Pompeii, during which they went up to the top of Vesuvius, 'and walked round the crater and watched the smoke and flame bursting up in the centre.'

The Rome visit had impressed Elizabeth and Maud considerably and they prevailed upon Robert to return there for the next winter. In the meantime their journeying continued in late April, when they left the growing heat of Naples for the more temperate Italian lakes which were always to be one of their favourite places. From there to Lugano in southern Switzerland was but a short step, at which they stayed until the third week in June, when they moved to the Hotel Monopol in Andermatt, the meeting place of the Oberalp, Furka and Gotthard Alpine passes. This high town was also known as the Aldershot of Switzerland, being a key military base guarding the frontier with Austria.

Robert obviously kept in touch with events back in Ireland, as in the 15th June copy of the *Belfast News Letter* he noticed the appointment of James Parkhill as President of the Methodist church in Ireland. He immediately penned a congratulatory letter to him, dated the 24th June: 'I see by a copy of the *News Letter* of the 15th inst the honours your brethren of the Ministry have conferred on you and I am glad to know of the high respect in which they must hold you to do so.'

Andermatt was left in the middle of October, when they returned to the Italian lakes, Lake Como this time, before the promised return to Rome. Maud's language skills had now reached a state where she could easily converse in either German, French or Italian '. . . to the club keepers, railway porters or anyone else we come across . . .', wrote Robert, adding 'she is thus a great help to us, as neither her mother or I know a word of any of these foreign languages.'

The Coeys settled in at the Hotel d'Italie in Rome, where they were to stay for some months. They were joined before Christmas by two of Maud's old school friends with their mother, from Newcastle-upon-Tyne. One of the girls was to stay on with them after Christmas, whilst the mother and other girl left to spend some time on the Riviera. Maud herself was still having Italian, music and painting lessons, in which her friends joined, together with their mother.

Rome was, to Robert, a city of great contrasts, wealth and poverty side-by-side in close juxtaposition. In an earlier letter from Rome he had identified the Vatican as an example of one of the few things described in guide books as exceeding his expectations, but did question the adequacy of the use made of it. 'Of the use that is made of it I am not so sure, as we never saw any adequate use made of it, a use that is in any way commensurate with its size and dignity while we were there.' His Methodist upbringing obviously made him question the need for such a flamboyant, complex and clearly expensive means to provide a place of worship and administration. Maud obviously relished such

A 2-10-2 electric locomotive of the Lotschberg Railway which would have taken trains through to Stresa in Italy via the Simplon Tunnel.   *Author's Collection*

Robert Coey in retirement at Harrogate (standing on right). Elizabeth seated in front, and Maud holding the cat at the back.   *Anne Parkhill*

places, as her Dublin upbringing had introduced her to the rich ritualistic services of the Roman Catholics.

The population of Rome had grown considerably over the past 50 years, from about 250,000 to some 700,000 and, like Florence, it was crowded at all times and not all that popular with Robert. What kept him there was his great interest in things architectural, particularly some of the palaces that abounded. His engineering mind acknowledged that the great feats of building construction achieved with the most basic of aids or tools were indeed marvels of their time.

It was probably around this time in Rome that Robert's brothers James, who had just retired from his General Managership of the NCC, and Henry, who was still employed by that concern, with their wives, came out to stay with Robert and Elizabeth, as Maud gleefully recounted in a letter: 'My Father's two brothers, also railway men, came out to stay with us in Rome in 1923 and my Mother asked them one day where they had been all day, and behold! They had spent the day in Rome Railway Station!'

Doubtless Robert would have pondered over some of the peculiarities of the Italian locomotives operating there, one class having external valve gear and inside cylinders and motion.

The following spring and summer were spent around their favourite haunts on the Italian lakes and in Switzerland, before returning to the Hotel d'Italie in Rome for a final Christmas. James and Adelaide Cowie returned for that time, and the party grew, with a Mrs and Miss Storey, the latter another of Maud's many schoolfriends joining them. Also a Miss Lockhart, from Newcastle, another of Maud's many friends came to swell the numbers.

Rome, at this time was preparing for the 1925 Holy Year celebrations and festival and accommodation was getting more expensive as the demand picked up. Robert therefore decided that, after four full years of travel, they would return to England.

So, in 1925, the Coeys came back to Harrogate and settled in at No. 61c, Kent Road, which was to be, so far as Robert was concerned, the last home. He enjoyed the remaining nine years left to him in this quiet part of the Duchy of Cornwall Estate. Coincidentally, James Marshall, with whose valve gear Coey had experimented back in 1904, lived nearby. Whether the two engineers met up socially in retirement is not known, but seems quite possible.

Maud settled in with her parents and involved herself in the Church of her choice, St Wilfrid's, where she became well-known for her flower-arranging and needlework skills, as well as her gardening and generous hospitality.

On 24th August, 1934, Robert passed away in Harrogate, at the good age of 83, and was cremated at Lawnswood, Leeds on the 27th. Elizabeth lived on until 1950, being cared for by Maud, when she joined Robert, having reached the age of 92. Maud continued living in Harrogate until 1993, deeply involved in caring for others and with her church, only agreeing to go into a home for the elderly in the last year or so of her life. She is still remembered with very great affection by those whose lives she touched.

We turn now to consider the careers of Robert's two younger brothers, James and Henry, both railwaymen of note in what was to become Northern Ireland.

James Cowie, a portrait photograph taken around 1905.   *Anne Parkhill*

Chapter Nine

James and Henry Cowie - Administrators
The Early Formative Years: 1855-1891

The three Coey/Cowie brothers were, possibly, unique in that they all chose the railway as a career path, although only Robert was to choose the engineering side, James and Henry settling for administration. James, born in 1855, when the family was living at No. 39, California Street, was to become a skilled administrator, preferring to manage affairs behind the engineering expertise, both civil and mechanical and, as such, be out of the limelight more commonly associated with engineering matters. Henry, some 20 years Robert's junior, also entered the railway scene, joining James on the administration side. He was born in 1871 at No. 17, Wilson Street, to which the family had moved from No. 23 some two years previously. Robert, we have seen, was a brilliant engineer who rose to high places in Dublin, yet the association with James and Henry seems to be missed, more particularly as he retained the Irish spelling Coey instead of the original Scottish name of Cowie adopted by James. James Cowie entered the office world in a very junior role and proved himself bright and resourceful enough to be marked out for promotion fairly early on in his chosen career of management.

In 1869, following his education in Belfast, whilst Robert was in the middle of his apprenticeship at the Lagan Foundry, James obtained a post of junior clerk on the staff of the General Manager of the Belfast & Northern Counties Railway, at a starting salary of £20 per year. He obviously showed himself capable of learning fast, and his expertise in administrative organisation grew by experience during these formative years. His salary had also doubled to £40 in a little over two years. The knowledge accumulated was stored up for future use and his natural abilities were noted by the General Manager, who ensured that he was kept informed of James' progress. It was to prove a good training ground, for he eventually was to rise through the ranks to the top position.

This General Manager who noticed James' abilities, was one Edward John Cotton, who, according to contemporary accounts, was the first really competent manager the railway had employed. His experience had been gained, firstly on the Great Western Railway and secondly at the Railway Clearing House in England, prior to becoming the Manager of the Waterford & Limerick Railway at the age of just 24. His move to the B&NCR in 1867 came at a crucial time in that railway's history, when it was struggling to achieve a satisfactory return on receipts. And, as so often in the case of good managers, Cotton recognised in James the makings of a future manager, and ensured that he was watched and guided to maximise his potential for the future.

Troubles in Ireland at this time, in that the odd Fenian gang was rampant and liable to shoot at personnel of important organisations without much warning, led Cotton, in 1872, to apply for a special licence to keep two 'single barrelled guns' in his office and make this fact widely known. A bit of over-reaction perhaps, but about three years later, Henry Ivatt, in his capacity of District Locomotive Superintendent at the Cork shed of the GS&WR kept a loaded revolver in the top drawer of his desk for the very same reason.

This 2-4-0 would have been in service when James started at York Road. No. 34 was built in 1861 by Beyer, Peacock.   *John Alsop Collection*

A relic of 1855, this 2-2-2T was in service for many years. Built by Fairbairn, it was withdrawn in 1898.   *John Alsop Collection*

By 1875 one of the B&NCR main routes, that to Londonderry, was fully upgraded following Cotton's instigation of the take-over of the Londonderry & Coleraine Railway in 1871, and further enhanced by the opening of a new station at Derry Waterside which replaced a rather poor, cramped station in 1875. This route between the two largest centres of population in Ulster, was to become one of the prime earners on the railway, even though it was in competition with the alternative Great Northern route via Omagh.

Matters under the steady and wise guidance of Cotton put the B&NCR in a good financial position, such that more expansion could be planned, initially by working two new railways bordering the B&NCR territory. These were the Derry Central Railway, opened in February 1880, and the Draperstown Railway, opened in July 1883. Both these additions were subsequently absorbed completely, the Derry Central in 1901 and the Draperstown in 1895.

Ireland had a number of narrow gauge developments as the final years of the 19th century approached. The first of these to be linked to the B&NCR was the Ballymena, Cushendall & Red Bay Railway. This 16½ mile line commenced operations in 1876, being then a strictly freight line to tap into the expanding iron ore trade which blossomed in that area. The B&NCR took it over completely in 1884, and immediately commenced passenger services to try and improve the receipts.

In 1885 there came a disturbing discovery by the Board. The company accountant, Hopkirk, together with his book-keeper, Lilley, were found to have embezzled over £16,000 of company funds between them. At the inevitable trial the means by which the money had disappeared was never fully discovered, such was the ingenuity of these two. Considerable damage was done to the company's name by this episode.

James by this time had been promoted to the upper echelons of the General Manager's staff, being given promotion to the position of Assistant to the General Manager in 1885 at the salary of £150. Additionally, Henry, the youngest Coey brother, joined the B&NCR as a junior clerk this year. James obviously had much to do with his brother's choice of the railway as a career and, of course, with Robert now firmly established on his way to the top at Inchicore, it was only natural for Henry to follow his peers choice of profession.

Where Robert and James were serious men, parsimonious in their speech and of a very rigid discipline where career was concerned, Henry, known as Harry within the family and to those close to him, on the other hand, had a totally different personality. 'The life and soul of the party' was a typical quote handed down through the family. Certainly his late arrival with three elder sisters around made him the 'baby' of the Coey household and it seems clear that the attention he would have got encouraged a friendly and generous nature. Most certainly the proceedings in the Manager's offices at York Road must have been enlivened after he started learning his trade there.

By 1886 Henry had moved to the position of clerk in the Stores Department, from where he was transferred into the Secretary's Department, a move which was to have a significant effect on his career in the early years of the next century. It is interesting to note that Henry is entered under the name 'Cowie' in the salaries book of the B&NCR, notably in James' handwriting! He may have wondered why James insisted on entering him as Cowie in the railway records, and indeed that spelling has been adopted by all those who have written about him in connection with the B&NCR - railway records having been the medium

B&NCR 0-6-0 No. 31. A pre-Malcolm design from Beyer, Peacock, this example lasted into the 1930s.

B&NCR 2-4-0 No. 1 of 1868. Two locomotives of this type were supplied by Beyer, Peacock and lasted (after rebuilds) until 1925.

B&NCR 2-4-0 No. 4. An 1871 rebuild of an original Bury 2-2-2 of 1847.

B&NCR 2-4-0 No. 22 of the 1872-1878 batch of nine engines from Beyer, Peacock.

Portrush station on 8th July, 1936.

John Alsop Collection

Portrush station building today.

Author

for the necessary research. However, his free and easy approach to life probably let him accept this without any fuss, although, outside the railway, he continued to use the Coey spelling for his personal affairs, as did James at this time. Whether James had visions of his younger brother stepping into his shoes later will never be known, but this might have been one reason to use the Cowie spelling associated with the railway. The days in which responsibilities were passed down through the family were to go, modern management was not to be structured that way, for large business concerns at least.

More involvements of the B&NCR in the narrow gauge field commenced in 1886, when Cotton undertook to advise the Ballycastle Railway, becoming effectively an unpaid Manager! His expertise obviously paid off, for in a few years this line was showing a healthy profit, a feature to elude many other narrow gauge concerns in Ireland. The Ballycastle had just over 16 miles of track and connected with the B&NCR main line at Ballymoney. The main receipts were dependent upon one main feature, this being the tourist and goods traffic to the seaside town of Ballycastle.

When Cotton was away advising on the Ballycastle affairs, James, in his capacity of Assistant, would have been in charge of the General Manager's Office. This gave him a good feel for the ultimate job of General Manager which did eventually come his way. One of the attributes of a good manager is the ability to delegate responsibility to others, and in this Cotton showed his hand in giving James the chance to prove his abilities - which he clearly did.

One further small concern with which the B&NCR had a close connection was to appear in 1883 as the Giant's Causeway, Portrush and Bush Valley Electric Tramway, when this initially opened as far as Bushmills. Commencing from outside Portrush station, this was the world's first hydro-electric railway and eased the journey of the tourists to the famous polygonal vertical rock formations east of Portrush which to this day attract many visitors. Its construction has been credited to the Traill brothers from Bushmills. William A.Traill was an engineering graduate of Trinity College, Dublin and Anthony Traill a Fellow of Trinity. The tramway project originated with William, who, with his brother, chose the London firm of Siemens to deal with the then revolutionary electrical side of things. On the whole, the hydro-electric system performed well, only causing some slight problems when water levels of the River Bush fell enough to cause some drop in the available current. This, however, was fairly predictable, and reversion to steam traction was sometimes required.

There were some peculiarities unique to this tramway. Firstly, for the initial ¾ mile, from Portrush station, the motive power was a steam tram engine. Outside Portrush the tram engine was uncoupled and the electric motors on the powered car took over, getting their current from a third rail, which was completely unprotected. The idea of leaving a live rail passing several hundred volts open to all beggars belief, but in those days electricity was more of a novelty than a commercial commodity requiring care in handling. The Act of Parliament passed in order to build this system apparently failed to include any clauses to prevent the current causing injuries to the public or animal life. Such injuries did occur, fatally in some cases involving livestock, and serious burns to those members of the public unaware of the warning notices posted at intervals. It was many years later that the current collection was altered to the

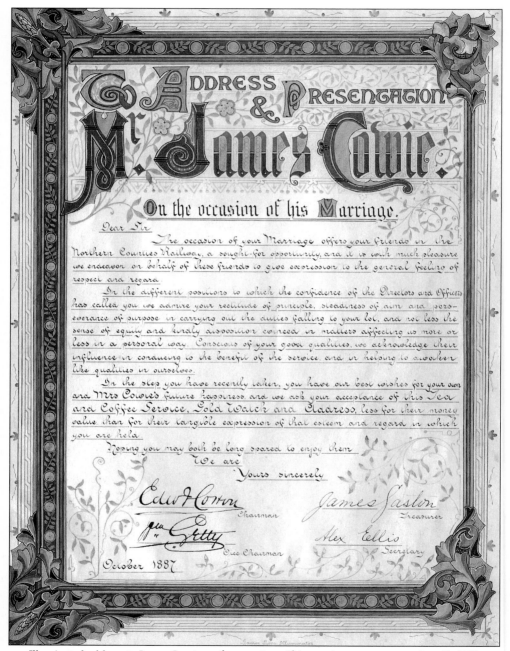

Illuminated address to James Cowie on the occasion of his marriage.

Anne Parkhill

safer overhead method, which then included the first short town portion, thus displacing the steam units.

Bushmills, famous for its whisky distillery, frequently sent its product for distribution by rail from Portrush. That lifelong teetotal Locomotive Superintendent of the B&NCR, Bowman Malcolm, whom we shall come across later, would certainly have raised his eyebrows at the thought of locomotives under his control and of his design being used for such a duty.

October 1887 brought marriage to Adelaide Thompson for James. The B&NCR staff, at a special gathering, presented him and his new bride with the gifts of a tea and coffee service and a gold watch together with a magnificent illuminated address, which latter still exists today and is illustrated opposite. Initially, the newly-weds set up home at No. 75, Limestone Road, Belfast which was very convenient for the Head Offices at York Road station. The following year James' salary was increased to £200, a generous sum in those days.

In October 1888, a new face appeared in the Civil Engineer's office. Berkeley Deane Wise joined the B&NCR from the Belfast & County Down Railway (B&CDR), replacing Robert Collins, who had resigned earlier that year. Wise was not only a thoroughly capable civil engineer, he was also a gifted architect, and this latter function was, in future years, to have a major effect on the railway's buildings throughout the province. However, his first task was to oversee the current programme of track renewal, with the old iron rails being progressively replaced by steel ones. A complete reballasting also took place, using stone from Whitehead.

Cotton used Wise and his skills to good advantage, and by the end of the 1890s, he and James Cowie had, at Wise's instigation, authorised the tablet system of single line working together with the introduction of the Manson tablet catcher. This latter apparatus, fitted to the locomotives, permitted trains to enter single line sections without stopping or slowing excessively, thus speeding schedules. For all of its existence, the B&NCR had extensive lengths of single track and any means of enhancing safety whilst offering time saving was obviously a benefit.

By 1889, James' involvement in yet more absorption of narrow gauge concerns came with the purchase of the Ballymena & Larne Railway. This railway, again 3 ft gauge, was opened in 1874 and was the first of such a gauge to carry passengers in Ireland. It also had the honour of running 'Boat Trains', the only such recorded occasion on a narrow gauge line in Ireland. The merging of all these external interests made sure that Edward Cotton and James Cowie were heavily engaged in the management of the growing concern which employed them.

In keeping with the other railways' excursions into the hotel sphere, the B&NCR opened the Northern Counties Hotel at the popular holiday resort of Portrush, to capitalise on the substantial seasonal tourist market there. The hotel itself had originally been known as the Antrim Arms, a well-known and established hostelry, and had been acquired by purchasing, in 1883, a £20,000 share in the lease. After much expenditure on enlargement and improvements, the hotel was purchased outright by the railway in 1891. Sadly, this establishment suffered a catastrophic fire in the 1970s and was destroyed. The site can still be seen today, open and undeveloped.

Painting of York Road station.

Anne Parkhill

York Road station on 6th July, 1936.

John Alsop Collection

Chapter Ten

Expansion and the death of Edward Cotton: 1891-1899

Considerable expansion of the York Road terminus in Belfast took place in the 1890s together with the building of the Station (later Midland) Hotel, an elegant structure sadly no longer with us, thanks to its virtual destruction during the German air raids on Belfast in 1941. This, together with subsequent redevelopment of that part of the city, has removed all trace of the station. The hotel had the distinction of being the first public building in Belfast to have electric lighting. Illustrated opposite is a picture of the York Road Terminus, painted in 1922 by J.W. Carey, a leading Irish landscape artist of the day. This formed part of an Album accompanying a presentation to James Cowie by the staff of the Traffic Department of the Midland Railway Company Northern Counties Committee (NCC) as the B&NCR had become, when he retired as Secretary and General Manager in 1922.

The reorganisation of the station was necessary to cope with the considerable increase in traffic, which, as the century came to a close was anticipated to grow further. The layout was revised by removing some sidings, building a new centre platform and adding a bay on the outside of the old arrival platform, giving five platforms in total. The concourse was rebuilt with new booking offices, bookstalls and refreshment facilities. Accompanying all this, the entire station had electric lighting installed. Signalling being the remit of the Civil Engineer's department Wise was charged with the complete resignalling of the revised station layout. In the ensuing exercise the most famous feature was the introduction of the 'somersault' type of semaphore signal, examples of which still exist today at Portrush station. The programme of development was completed one month before the Station Hotel opened for business.

One feature of the York Road terminus was the fact that it was an interesting construction exercise, built on reclaimed land on the banks of Belfast Lough. The main buildings were carried on piles driven down to the bedrock and, being about a mile from the city centre proper, were connected to this by the Belfast Corporation tramcars, once these were established in their horse-drawn status, to be updated to electric operation as that medium became available. It was the second largest of the three main line terminals in the city, the Great Victoria Street station of the Great Northern being the largest.

The rebuilding of York Road terminus was not the only renewal programme carried out by the railway, as Wise had already dealt with Portrush station, which is still a noteable feature in that town. Many more stations were to be planned or renewed before the end of the century by his architectural exercises, notably, those at Larne Harbour, Greenisland, Carrickfergus, Trooperslane, Antrim, Ballymoney and Ballymena as well as the Portstewart Tramway Depot.

There was a further crucial aspect of the B&NCR operations which was the all-important shipping connection with the mainland. Shortly after James commenced his employment the railway was involved in the relaunch of the Larne-Stranraer boat service. This had been briefly operated between 1862-63

One of the last paddle steamers serving Larne, the *Princess Victoria*.   *John Alsop Collection*

Larne quay and passenger station in July 1936.   *John Alsop Collection*

but had been withdrawn due to poor returns. The recommencement in 1872 by the Larne and Stranraer Steamboat Company, which was encouraged by Cotton, proved considerably more successful. This service between Scotland and Northern Ireland, apart from the abortive Portpatrick-Donaghadee service, was the shortest sea crossing between the two countries, and has run ever since. By 1891 a mail packet service was established under contract to the Post Office. From 1875 two paddle steamers, the *Princess Louise* and *Princess Beatrice* were in service, to be replaced by the *Princess Victoria* and *Princess May* by 1892, again paddle steamers. The approach to Stranraer was shallow and dictated the need for paddle steamers with their low draught for the first 30 years of the service. In 1893, the shipping company designation and structure was changed to the Larne and Stranraer Steamship Joint Committee. This Committee comprised of representatives from the LNWR, Caledonian Railway, Glasgow & South Western Railway (G&SWR), Midland Railway, Portpatrick & Wigtownshire Railway and the B&NCR. James Cowie became the B&NCR representative, his salary being increased to £300 shortly after. His company's involvement in this shipping route, which provided a quick connection between two of the main population centres of Scotland and Ireland, Glasgow and Belfast, was to be just one of the deciding factors in the Midland Railway's decision to take over the line later.

One of the best sources of revenue for the B&NCR, apart from the regular commuter services to and from Belfast, was the tourist market. With the Stranraer to Larne shipping service well established, Cotton began some publicity to attract tourist trade in the North of Ireland. He and James spent many hours planning a poster campaign, backed up with illustrated guide books describing the places served by their railway. The posters were to be found all over the railway system on the mainland as well as in hotels and golf clubhouses. Representation of the B&NCR was to be found far from Ireland in the mid-1890s, with displays at the Chicago World Fair and Antwerp Universal Exhibition to give a couple of examples. Many cheap excursion fares were offered in connection with the tourist trade, which attracted not only those from other parts of the UK but were widely used by the local population at holidays and weekends.

For such a small concern to be heavily engaged in publicising its services so widely was unique in those days, yet from this the prosperity of the railway grew as the impact of the tourist trade (albeit seasonal) began to be felt. For the reasonably limited investment involved, the return was considerable.

Considerable investment in new locomotives and stock took place in parallel with the expansion of the B&NCR. The major feature, so far as locomotives were concerned, was the introduction by Bowman Malcolm of the compound locomotive to the Irish scene in 1890, just before Ivatt and Robert Coey at Inchicore began their experiments in that field. Malcolm had attained the position of Locomotive Superintendent as far back as 1875 at the age of just 22, and was to persist very successfully on the compound theme for many more years.

Records at the Belfast City cemetery list the names of the burials of three infants, James Thompson Coey, Adelaide Frances Coey and Hubert Coey. Their

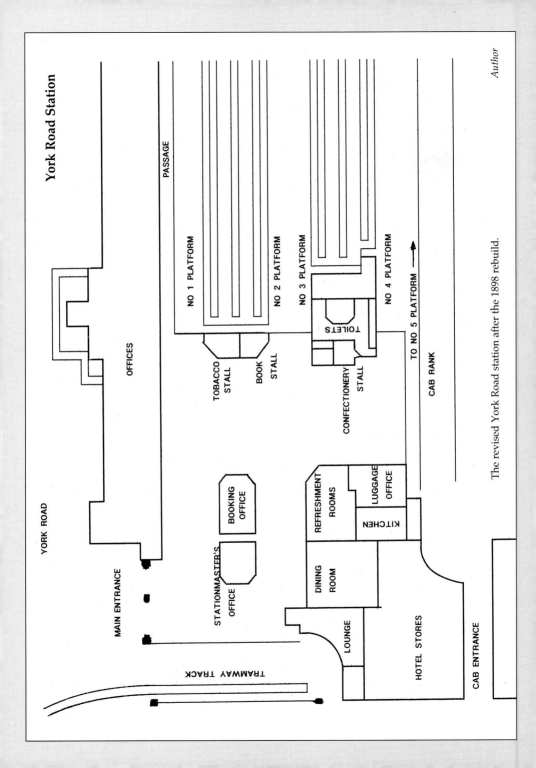

York Road Station

The revised York Road station after the 1898 rebuild.

Author

ages were 3 weeks, 7 months and 8 days respectively. The dates of death are given as 18th August, 1890, 21st July, 1893 and 8th December, 1893. These three children were born to Adelaide Cowie and it appears that she and James went through two years of tragic happenings. The causes of death are not known, but high infant mortality was then on the decline which certainly would have compounded the parent's grief. It says much that their graves are unmarked. It also says much for James' character that he did not allow this situation to undermine his career. His parents and other members of the family were to hand to help him and Adelaide through their sorrow.

Robert, in Dublin, was, as we have seen earlier, to go through the loss of his first child in 1894, and the family as a whole felt the shock of the multiple tragedies of the early 1890s, undoubtedly being sustained by their deep Christian faith.

August 1897 saw a flurry of activity in the Manager's office and at York Road works to prepare a Royal Train for the forthcoming visit of the Duke and Duchess of York to Ireland. The B&NCR had the responsibility of transporting the Royal party from Londonderry to Newtownards on 4th September. The brand-new 4-4-0 No. 60, delivered a month previously from Beyer, Peacock, headed the special train.

By the end of the century, the B&NCR was in a good financial position. The stalwart efforts of Cotton and Cowie were beginning to show the benefits of their careful planning in the form of good receipts for both commuters and tourists alike. For a relatively small railway, never more than 250 track miles up to now, including the narrow gauge acquisitions, the profitability of its services was fast becoming a legend. James' salary had by this time risen to £400, a good amount for those days. York Road terminus had an intensive service, emphasis being given to the needs of the rush-hour in addition to the Larne boat expresses and Portrush and Londonderry lines. At the height of the summer holiday season, the Portrush expresses were frequently run in as many as four portions, such was the demand for transport to the seaside.

However, a significant new development was taking place on the Midland Railway in England which was to influence events on the Northern Counties when, following a short illness, Edward Cotton died on 11th June, 1899. His General Managership had lasted 32 years, one of the longest on record, and had placed the railway in the top league so far as efficiency and profits were concerned. His wise guidance and selection of key personnel through the years had moulded the management team into a well-integrated mix of skills.

Joseph Tatlow, of B&CDR and Midland Great Western managership, wrote of Cotton:

In railway circles throughout England, Scotland and Ireland he was widely known. He attended all railway conferences, for he loved travel and movement. Shrewd and well-informed, his knowledge was acquired not from books or study but from close observation of passing events and free and friendly intercourse with all whom he met. His railway was very popular and he and it were held in high esteem.

Such was the measure of the man James Cowie was now appointed to replace.

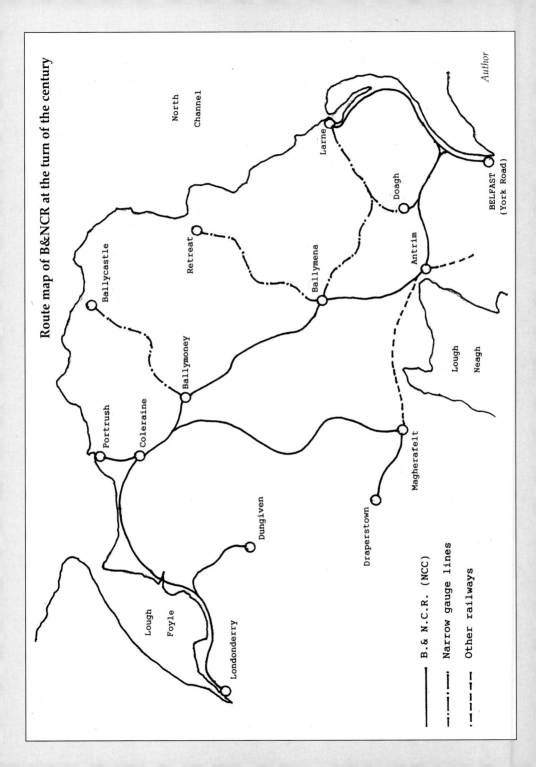

Route map of B&NCR at the turn of the century

North
Channel

Ballycastle

Retreat

Ballymena

Larne

Doagh

Antrim

BELFAST
(York Road)

Lough
Neagh

Ballymoney

Portrush

Coleraine

Dungiven

Magherafelt

Draperstown

Lough
Foyle

Londonderry

Author

B.& N.C.R. (NCC)

Narrow gauge lines

Other railways

Whilst all this dramatic upheaval had been occupying James' time, Henry had married Margaret Knox and with this marriage, all the children of James senior and Sarah had found their spouses.

One expansion exercise of the B&NCR which was ongoing when Cotton died, was the long drawn-out series of negotiations and counter-arguments regarding the Derry Central Railway (DCR). This line connected the existing Northern Counties main line to Coleraine and Londonderry with the Cookstown branch and thus offered an alternative route from Belfast to those places. From the outset the B&NCR worked the DCR for a percentage of the receipts. It never was a profitable line, much of the receipts left after paying the B&NCR percentage going to cover the interest charges on the Board of Works loans obtained during the construction of the line.

By the middle of 1899 matters were still moving gradually towards an eventual take-over and, following Cotton's death, James found much of his time being absorbed in the protracted negotiations by then well under way. Much of the final dealings were taken in hand by the B&NCR Chairman, the Rt Hon. John Young who, despite his 75 years, finally reached an agreement with the Treasury in London on the price to be paid to the Board of Works so that the DCR debt could be written off. Young managed to get his Board to agree to provide £20,000, on top of the £85,000 for the Board of Works, which enabled the DCR shareholders to receive 4s. 6d. in the pound.

A wedding photograph of Henry Cowie. The mists of time have faded the identities of the other parties present. Henry and bride on the left. *Anne Parkhill*

Therefore, on 4th April, 1901, the Board of Works took possession of the DCR and passed it on to the B&NCR. It was not until 17th August that the Act covering this amalgamation was granted Royal Assent, this giving the B&NCR full possession of the line. James was immensely relieved that this lengthy business was over. This left him free to concentrate more fully on the lengthy negotiations associated with the on-coming merger with the Midland Railway, which was to be the main topic of business over the next two years.

James, as has already been mentioned, was in temperament and demeanour, very similar to his elder brother Robert. A studious and serious person, his knowledge of railway working was, by now, wide-ranging, which made sure that his promotion to General Manager was a foregone conclusion. His application to his work was meticulous and those receiving orders from him would have known that these were soundly based. Most certainly they would have had the best interests of the railway, its customers and the staff behind them.

We need now to look in some detail at the happenings over the next crucial two decades, when a take-over, a war and Irish politics altered matters drastically for the fortunes of the railways in Ireland, concentrating on the B&NCR scene and James' and Henry's involvements in that.

The 2-4-0ST, No. 49. One of a class of four originally built as a side tank and converted in 1891.   *R.G. Jarvis/MRT*

Chapter Eleven

The Years of Change:
1899-1906

The death of Edward Cotton was a grievous loss to the B&NCR. However, James had been nurtured by Cotton as a potential successor and so it was merely a matter of course that the Board approved his promotion to the now vacant position of General Manager.

There were, however, two small rays of hope in these early days of the new century, firstly in that the Coey/Cowie families rejoiced at the safe arrival of Robert and Elizabeth's second daughter, Maud, with James and Henry both congratulating their brother and his wife on this late, but welcome addition to the family. Secondly, Henry and Margaret were delighted with the arrival of their daughter, Mabel Sarah in 1902. After so many disappointments of the earlier years in the family, these two healthy girls brought immense happiness. Henry, in particular, would have fallen into fatherhood with great pleasure, as he always enjoyed the company of children. His duties would probably have been limited to companionship and story-telling as was the accepted custom of the time. The more mundane matters of child care such as bathing and nappy-changing were left to the nannies and, occasionally, the mothers in middle-class circles.

As the above events were unfolding, across in England the Board of the Midland Railway were searching around for a suitable Irish railway to add to their current empire. They had recently invested in a new port at Heysham to service their new sea routes to the Isle of Man and Ireland. As the Irish steamer route was to be to Belfast it was logical to consider purchasing a railway operating from that city. The B&NCR, with its connections to Londonderry and the holiday resorts on the North Antrim coast, fitted the bill perfectly, more particularly due to its current profitability. In 1901-2 early approaches were made to the B&NCR Board regarding an outright sale of the complete railway and all its accessories. The negotiations that ensued were complex, and James found himself heavily engaged in them as time progressed. The take-over was agreed in principle, and many months of hard work for James lay ahead connected with the transfer of management from the existing Board to a Committee of Management, known as the 'Northern Counties Committee' which was to be based in Belfast. The Act authorising the take-over consisted of 31 clauses, covering 16 pages, with one particular clause (No. 26) covering the absorption of the Limavady & Dungiven Railway, of which we shall read more later in connection with Henry.

The financial side of matters agreed for the take-over was that the existing ordinary shares in the B&NCR were to be exchanged for Midland Railway ordinary and preference shares, the MR offering a fixed dividend rather than the variable dividend associated with the B&NCR. The total capitalisation was £2,153,838. The NCC would have no capital of its own, all matters of capital outlay being sanctioned by the Derby Board, and all revenue from the Irish operation was handed over to the Midland. The purchase of the B&NCR was funded from new Midland stock raised in 1903, the dividends of which were paid from the NCC revenue. So, in some ways, the relationship between Belfast and Derby had a few similarities to the devolution system imposed on Northern Ireland within the United Kingdom in 1921.

At the winding up of the B&NCR as a separate railway, out of the balance of £40,000 surplus funds available, £4,500 was put aside for distribution amongst the six principal officers. James, as one of the two most senior received at least £700, probably more, a substantial sum for those days.

Accordingly, on 1st July, 1903, the Midland Railway took over the B&NCR. James remained as General Manager, there being no reason to replace him, his expertise in running the affairs of the railway was well known and enabled matters to transfer smoothly from one management structure to another. The Committee, to whom James reported, was made up of three Board members from York Road and three from Derby. The MR initially had little influence on the stock situation of the B&NCR. The existing locomotives and stock together with new additions remained for some years based on the designs of Bowman Malcolm, who had served as Chief Engineer and Locomotive Superintendent since 1876, one of the longest serving such persons in the British Isles. Bowman Malcolm and James Cowie had worked closely together throughout many of those years since 1876 and their respect for each other's capabilities went a long way towards the smooth running of the railway. Even the long-established green livery of the locomotives remained unchanged for many years after the take-over.

By this time Robert Coey was embarking on his journey to America to gather information on the state-of-the-art in locomotive developments in the United States, in case recourse had to be made to obtain new stock from the builders in that land.

Whilst the negotiations for the take-over were being formulated, matters did not rest, for James was busy organising the introduction of a fleet of road vehicles to improve the transit of goods to and from from the yards around the railway. Initially steam powered, these lorries were soon to be augmented by internal combustion powered units, and replaced many of the earlier horse-drawn vehicles. As far back as 1898, the importance of marrying road and rail transport of goods had been noted by Cotton, resulting in the purchase of a 6 hp Milne-Daimler van to assess the potential. James, on becoming General Manager had repalced the Whiteabbey and Greenisland horse buses by two Thorneycroft 24 hp steam buses in 1902. This constituted the first railway-owned mechanically-propelled bus service in the British Isles. Touring buses were soon added to the road fleet, stationed at the popular resorts on the Antrim coast served by the NCC, enabling holidaymakers to visit many of the outlying towns which did not benefit from a railway connection. Committee members were given a taste of the possibilities as to tourist revenue by taking a demonstration trip around the Antrim Coast Road. Their mode of transport was a Milne-Daimler 16 seat charabanc powered by a four-cylinder engine. James, along with William Wise, the Secretary, and Bowman Malcolm, accompanied them. The trip started at Larne and went to Portrush via Glenarm, Cushendall and Ballycastle. After spending the night at Portrush some local sightseeing was made, taking in Dunluce, the Giant's Causeway and Carrick-a-Rede, followed by a return to Belfast by special train. These early pioneering introductions showed that the B&NCR (NCC) was aware that road transport could add to the railway's business and that it was a considerably cheaper than building branch lines.

The NCC began with an update of the Larne-Stranraer shipping fleet by the Shipping Committee. Out went the dated paddle steamers, modern shallow draught vessels now being available. The steamer *Princess Maud* arrived from the Clydeside shipbuilders Denny's to swell the fleet on this route. The vessel was 300 feet long and had a beam of 40 feet with a gross tonnage of 1,746. It was also the first Irish Sea ship to have turbine power, then in its early days, giving a speed of some 20 knots. The new Belfast-Heysham route of the Midland was served by three new ships, the *Antrim*, *Donegal* and *Londonderry*, and whilst these were supplied and run by the Midland Railway, the NCC was involved in providing the support and docking facilities at Belfast's Donegal Quay.

In concert with the shipping reorganisation, the MR introduced a through train to Stranraer to connect with the Larne sailings. The train concerned left St Pancras at 8.30 pm. However, with entry to Ireland still possible via many other routes this connection was not very much used and, by 1910, had been altered to some sleeping cars on the Glasgow night express, these being detached at Dumfries. Additionally, the MR had, in 1904, opened the Heysham route, so it was hardly likely that the Stranraer route would be a front runner, despite its shorter journey time. The real importance of Stranraer to Larne was not to come until partition in 1921.

One of James's many responsibilities in his top job concerned sorting out arguments between other Irish railways which arose on the matter of traffic receipts. A typical example arose in 1904 when, following the merger of the Waterford, Limerick & Western Railway (WL&WR) into the Great Southern & Western Railway, the Midland Great Western Railway objected to the GS&WR apportionment of traffic receipts for goods routed over the absorbed WL&WR from Collooney, Swinford and Claremorris for export to England via Dublin which passed over its lines. They desired a split more in keeping with the new situation. A dispute arose between the GS&WR and MGWR which, after much protracted argument, was put out for arbitration. James Cowie, being an impartial party to this dispute, was duly appointed as arbitrator. He was sent, in early 1904, the documents containing the allegations and arguments of the two railways for his judgement in this matter. On the 10th March that year his findings were published, in that the MGWR was to receive 1s per ton and the GS&WR 1s. 6d. per ton terminal charges, with the balance of traffic receipts for the Irish part of the journey to be apportioned in proportion to the mileage travelled on the two railways. Following this judgement the two railways involved ended their dispute and accepted James' ruling.

During 1904, the health of William Gill, who had been Secretary of the B&NCR since 1887, took a turn for the worse and he retired on 1st January, 1905. James Cowie assumed his responsibilities and took the title General Manager and Secretary. His salary was increased to £800 per year to account for this change. However, the extra workload meant that Cowie had to relinquish his position on the steamship committee, being replaced by one William McConchie.

In October 1904 James proposed that the service between Greenisland and Antrim would benefit from a frequent railmotor service. This route passed through much of the Belfast suburbs and it was thought that better patronage would ensue. Steam railmotors were, at this time, all the rage all over the British Isles and the Midland works at Derby provided two examples for the NCC. New halts were built at Monkstown, Ballyrobert and Muckamore expressly for the planned service. However, the Traffic Department put these new vehicles in service on the Belfast to Ballymena route and expected these low-powered motors to haul extra vans. Needless to say they were most unsuitable for this and rapidly became worn out. By 1913 they were withdrawn and scrapped. If they had been rigidly employed on the suburban runs, they might well have lasted many more years and possibly resulted in the further introduction of diesel railmotors already, by 1910, in evidence on some of the narrow gauge lines in Ireland.

A year after James took on Secretary's responsibilities, Berkeley Wise retired. He had been ill for some time and was actually on six months leave of absence when, in September of 1906, he decided to resign completely as his health was 'of such a nature that he cannot resume his duties . . .' And so departed a capable and popular figure. He died less than three years later at the age of 56. Malcolm assumed the responsibilities for civil engineering , a position he retained until retirement. The old guard were fading fast, only Cowie and Malcolm remained of the top management which had lifted the B&NCR to the levels it had enjoyed before the take-over.

Whilst all this had been going on, the final events in the saga of the Limavady & Dungiven Railway (L&D) were coming to a close. This 10 mile branch line extension followed the valley of the River Roe, which had its source in the Sperrin mountains, and had been operated by the B&NCR since opening in 1883, some five years after the Act authorising its construction. From inception this line was plagued with financial problems, the B&NCR subscribing no less than £58,000 capital plus a mortgage of £25,000 over the five years. Much of the other capital required came from the Irish Board of Works as loan capital at 4 per cent interest. The basic agreement was that the B&NCR would work the line for 10 years for 70 per cent of the receipts. From the first the receipts were poor, rarely exceeding £1,100 in any one half-year, and the L&D staggered on, with interest due accumulating at a prodigious rate. By 1905, after the formation of the NCC, a move was made to strengthen the L&D connection. Following the death of that line's Secretary, David Hamilton, Henry Cowie was appointed to the post by brother James, who had assumed the managership of the L&D on becoming General Manager of the B&NCR and was in a good position to monitor and advise on the progress of negotiations. Henry had now been in the employ of the B&NCR (NCC) for some 18 years, mainly in the Secretary's Office, slowly but steadily working his way through the administrative ranks. Never as gifted as James, his outgoing personality made him a popular figure both socially and at work. This appointment was, politically, a wise one on the part of James, for some delicate negotiations were to start in connection with the complete take-over of the L&D.

Henry was immediately engaged in preparations for the NCC's take-over of the bankrupt railway, the debts now owing to the Board of Works exceeding £30,000. When the Midland Railway had taken over the B&NCR a clause had been inserted in the agreement for the settlement of the L&D situation by arbitration - it was this procedure that Henry now instigated.

By late 1906, matters had progressed to a point where a special general meeting of the Board of the L&D was called. This took place at Limavady on the 26th November. Henry Cowie described the negotiations he had had with the Board of Works and the NCC concerning the proposed purchase and authorisation to close the deal was given, although the shareholders' recompense was minimal.

Thus after almost a full year's negotiations the L&D was fully in the possession of the NCC from February 1907 after the payment to the Lords' Commissioners of HM Treasury and the Board of Works of the sum of just £2,000! Henry returned to James' department after this short, but important, episode in his career. The complex negotiations connected with the L&D episode were certainly helped by Henry's easygoing personality.

James saw his brother Robert occasionally, keeping him in touch with developments in the North, as he was now the NCC representative of the Irish Railway Managers Conference (IRMC), which met regularly in Dublin. His trips down to attend the meetings permitted him to visit Robert at Inchicore and his home after the matters of business had been disposed of at the IRMC. Robert was busily engaged in his express locomotive developments and also bringing out his first large 4-6-0 goods locomotives.

Narrow gauge expansion continued in 1906, when the NCC became involved with the County Donegal Railway (CDR). The CDR had, in 1900, opened an extension of some 14½ miles from Strabane to Londonderry, where they built a terminus, Victoria Road, adjacent to the Carlisle bridge. This particular extension was, incredibly, parallel to the existing GNR line from Strabane to Londonderry, and provided a competitive journey. The completion of this line brought the CDR mileage up to 124½, the largest narrow gauge line in Ireland. The MR still wished to add to its Irish railways and began to make moves to take over the CDR, which by now was in a precarious financial state. However, the GNR raised vigorous opposition, as they had quite substantial traffic derived from the CDR, and to have the NCC tap a substantial amount of this off was not to be tolerated. Acrimonious debate followed, with Parliament finally ruling that any take-over was to be a joint affair, the CDR was to be jointly transferred to the GNR and MR(NCC). In line with the 1903 MR takeover of the B&NCR there was to be a joint committee of management - the County Donegal Railways Joint Committee (CDRJC) - to consist of three nominees of each company. Back at York Road, James would have actively promoted this take-over, as the CDRJC lines ran through some of the most spectacular countryside in Ireland. The tourist potential through connections to Belfast appeared considerable.

In Cotton's days (in 1870) a scheme of 'villa tickets' had been instigated, and had proved very successful in attracting business to the railway. These were, in essence, a free first class ticket to and from Belfast valid for 10 years, and were

County Donegal Joint narrow gauge 4-6-4T No. 10 *Owenea* at Strabane on 14th May, 1937.
R.G. Jarvis/MRT

A CDJR 2-6-4T No. 17 *Glenties* at Strabane, in excellent condition.   *R.G. Jarvis/MRT*

granted to anyone building a 'villa' of annual poor law valuation of £25 or more. The main proviso was that these were within a mile of any station between Belfast and Larne. This scheme, over the years, encouraged the development of suburbs of Belfast such as Jordanstown and Carrickfergus and, in particular, the town of Whitehead from very small beginnings. The latter town, located on the north shore of Belfast Lough a few miles east of Carrickfergus, benefited considerably from the railway, which allowed it to become a desired residential and holiday resort. The promenade, in fact, was constructed with the financial backing of the railway in 1901. As the town's popularity grew, in 1907 James ordered that a large supplementary island platform be built adjacent to the existing station to accommodate the special trains run during the summer months and on public holidays.

An extra responsibility came James way over the years 1906 to 1909, in that he was busy preparing evidence to present before the Vice-Regal Commission on Irish Railways on behalf of the NCC. Discussions were taking place regarding the possibility of merging some, or all, of the railways in Ireland. If this had actually happened, the problems raised by the partition to come in the 1920s would have been considerable. As it was, with the slow progress made, the Commission never got round to any hard and fast recommendations, and was eventually to be overtaken by events as war approached.

A relic from the past. On the approach to Portrush station this somersault signal still stands in 2002 as a reminder of early days.   *Author*

Chapter Twelve

Prosperity, War and the Aftermath: 1906-1919

Many of the smaller railway companies in Ireland, particularly the narrow gauge ones, were in a precarious financial state and, clearly, something had to be done. The preliminary report of the Vice-Regal Commission came down strongly in favour of the unification of all railways and that this recommendation be put to Westminster. However, no resolute action was tabled to put the case forward to Parliament and thus matters remained until World War I started. The political arena in Ireland was changed permanently by the happenings during and after that event.

The NCC had acquired an exemplary record so far as industrial relations were concerned. The B&NCR had always had a good management/employee accord, in many respects due to the comprehensive welfare arrangements it had set up. These consisted of a Provident Society, a Pension Fund and a Savings Bank in addition to a Widows and Orphans Fund and a Chairman's Fund. The Widows and Orphans Fund was enhanced by a 1908 ruling by James that it should benefit from money taken in staff fines plus any unclaimed money found in trains. The Chairman's Fund was created to provide money from which individual cases of hardship experienced by the families of employees could be alleviated. All these arrangements had been absorbed into the NCC.

The 19th February, 1910 produced one of the few major accidents to blot the NCC's copybook. The 6.25 pm Stranraer Boat Express, consisting of 4-4-0 No. 62 with two mail vans, three coaches and guard's brake, was derailed at speed after running into a landslip which occurred in the late afternoon at Briggs Loop near Whitehead. The early twilight had prevented earlier trains from seeing the onset of the landslip and warning the signalmen. The engine stayed upright perched precariously on the edge of the trackbed, which at this point was beside the sea. The carriages, however, came completely off the track and fell into the sea, which at that point fortunately was shallow. Apart from some considerable shock and a wetting none of the passengers was seriously injured. This area had been notorious for landslips which had caused the line to be closed for a day each time in December 1908 and February 1909. Cowie and Malcolm quickly had some remedial work carried out to eliminate, so far as possible, the risk of further trouble.

Amongst Cowie's many tasks was that of representing the NCC at conferences. One such venue was the International Railway Congress, which in 1910, was held in Berne, Switzerland. Both James and Bowman Malcolm were listed as the delegates at this Congress but, according to the records, never attended. James was heavily engaged in his dual role of Secretary and General Manager, whilst Malcolm was busy fulfilling his dual civil and mechanical engineering duties.

Typical of James Cowie's handling of the wages situation for the NCC staff is the example of 1911, when porters demanded a rise of 2s. per week, being granted 1s. in July of that year. This prompted the shunters to claim a similar rise, which was granted in September, it also being made applicable to the signalmen on Cowie's instructions thus alleviating a certain follow-on claim by them. Passenger guards also had their wages increased by amounts between 2s. and 4s. depending upon grade, the goods guards/brakemen benefiting by 1s. to 3s., again according to grade. The manner in which James had handled these demands was much appreciated by the workers involved, who sent a letter to the Board to the effect that the good employee/management relations might continue to be 'even more firmly established'.

The continued good relations encouraged by James over the years of his managership lead to a railway largely free of industrial disputes. The Board decided in 1911 to grant unpaid leave of absence to as many employees as could be released on the Coronation Day of Edward VII. Those who had to remain at work were either given an extra day's pay or an extra day's holiday later that year.

The good industrial relations engendered by the above paid dividends twice later in 1911. Firstly, in August, the British railways were affected by a strike. The NCC remained fully operational, its employees ignoring repeated calls by representatives of the other railways' employees for their support. For this steadfastness they received three day's extra pay. Also from 20th September to 5th October the vast majority of Irish railways, the Midland Great Western, Great Southern & Western, Great Northern and Belfast & County Down were all crippled by a serious strike. The NCC employees remained at work, being granted an extra week's pay for this demonstration of loyalty.

As a result of all this, James Cowie received a salary increase to £1,000 that year and the fortunes of the company prospered. That salary level represents roughly £45,000 in today's (1998) terms.

In 1910-11 the shipyard of Harland and Wolff, one of the largest industrial employers in Ireland, was very busy. The huge bulks of the *Olympic* and *Titanic* were rising in sequence above the tightly packed houses bordering the yard. At that time the largest passenger ships in the world, on 20th October, 1910 the *Olympic* slid majestically into the waters of Belfast Lough. Alongside rose the second hull of the *Titanic* which was to become famous for its first, and only, voyage, on which it struck an iceberg and sank taking two-thirds of the passengers and crew with it.

The *Titanic* launch took place on 31st May, 1911, watched by a huge crowd, many of whom had travelled by train to Belfast to view the launching, which had been well publicised beforehand. The spectacle was enhanced by the presence of the completed *Olympic*, which sailed that very afternoon for Liverpool, where she was open for public inspection, and then on to Southampton to commence Atlantic service. The chance to see the two largest passenger ships in the World side-by-side was unique. Extra transport for these onlookers had been organised by the railway companies in conjunction with the Belfast Corporation Tramways, which ferried many of the thousands from the stations to Queen's Island. As with the *Olympic* before, the *Titanic* was towed to the dockside for the final sumptuous fitting out by hundreds of craftsmen, which took some nine months of effort. The extensive dockyard railway system, to which the NCC was connected by a spur from York Road, was busy as its

A period postcard view of the Titanic as she nears completion in Belfast.

The *Olympic*, sister ship of the ill-fated *Titanic*, which was modified with higher water-tight bulkheads. At Southampton in the 1920s.   *R.G. Jarvis Collection*

small locomotives fussed around moving supplies and materials to be swallowed up by these masterpieces of shipbuilding expertise. Clearly visible from many vantage points around the city, the twin vessels seemed to symbolise the pinnacle of ship construction which had given Belfast a reputation for quality.

It was shortly after this unique event in Belfast that Robert retired from the GS&WR in Dublin and departed for England, never to return permanently to Ireland.

As 1912 approached James learnt of his appointment as Chairman of the Irish Railway Managers Conference which met regularly throughout the year. In this capacity he presided at the farewell banquet held for Joseph Tatlow on 9th January in Dublin. Tatlow had brought order and profitability to the Belfast and County Down and Midland Great Western companies in succession during a very distinguished career as General Manager of those lines, and was regarded by many in railway circles as a figurehead.

The political situation in Ireland was becoming unsettled, with the Republican movement growing in intensity and purpose, particularly as Asquith's Home Rule Bill of 1912 was going through Westminster. This Bill specified a united Ireland, within the United Kingdom, ruled from Dublin. Ulster was not listed for separate treatment and it was obvious that this prosperous province with its Protestant majority would never submit to Catholic Dublin.

The Ulster Volunteer Force (UVF), formed by those opposing Home Rule, and the Unionist hierarchy liaised with the railways in Ulster, drawing up contingency plans to prevent the movement of troops by rail into the Province should the British Government force matters. To this end a demonstration of the UVF potential was made on 24th April, 1914 when 1,000 of its members occupied York Road station and effectively prevented any train movements taking place.

As it stood the Bill failed, being thrown out by the Lords in January 1913, and by the time it had been repassed over their heads under the Parliament Act, World War I had broken out and the matter was submerged temporarily in the events overshadowing the country.

The growth of the B&NCR (NCC) up to 1913 is worth considering. The increases in traffic and receipts compared to the 1902 values - the last full year of independence for the railway - were considerable under James' continued managership, with passenger numbers increasing by no less than 14 per cent and goods by 19 per cent. The corresponding receipts increased by 21 per cent and 20 per cent respectively. By 1913, nearly 4 million passengers and almost 900,000 tons of freight were dealt with each year, the total profits being £453,000. For a railway having a total route mileage of just 265 miles in a province containing a little over 1 million people these figures were impressive. However, further examination of the data available reveals a sharp increase in working expenses of some 39 per cent. Some problems, then, obviously lay ahead, but before James and his team could apply themselves to resolve them, war had broken out and normal management techniques had to be sidelined.

The Parkhill wedding in Cork. The well-educated status of the Coey/Parkhill families is emphasised by the number of clerical collars in view (four). Henry is to be found standing second from the left with Margaret beside him. Their daughter, Sally, is seated on the ground front right. The two Parkhill (née Coey) sisters are seated. Mary the bride's mother, third from the right and Catherine far right. Robert Parkhill is to be found seated third from the left. The house in the background is the Parkhill home in Cork, Beaumont House, the favourite of Maud Coey.

Anne Parkhill

In late April 1913, Henry and his family travelled down to Cork to attend the wedding of his niece, Lilian Parkhill, no doubt sampling the GS&WR motive power of brother Robert on the way. The bride's father, Robert Parkhill, was, as we have seen in Chapter Seven, a well-respected businessman in that area. Sadly, only a few months later, in December of that year, he collapsed and died very suddenly of a brain haemorrhage. Both Henry and James travelled down to Cork for the funeral and to support their sister Mary in her great loss. Henry would have reflected on the happy occasion of his previous visit, and his kind and generous nature would have been directed towards his grieving sister to complement the support of James.

On 24th August, 1914, as the British Expeditionary Force was pouring across the Channel to France to try and help stem the German advance through Belgium, and the United Kingdom geared up for an exhausting war which was not only to change Europe but the railway scene throughout the lands, James Coey senior died in his 89th year. After the funeral and interment at Belfast City Cemetery the family rallied round Sarah and she lived on at No. 5 The Glen, off the Limestone Road, the house that had been her home for 30 years. In 1915, at the good age of 90, she too died and was buried beside her beloved and faithful James in the family plot in the City Cemetery.

In Great Britain the outbreak of war resulted in the Government taking control of all the railways on the mainland; but those in Ireland did not, until 1917, come under the control of the Board of Trade which then acted through a supervisory committee of five managers of the largest railways concerned, the Irish Railways Executive Committee (IREC). James was immediately selected as one of the five for this committee for the duration. He was also awarded a £100 increase in his salary, to £1,300, in June of that year.

The effect of the war on the NCC was slight, compared to the railways in the South which were particularly badly affected as some friction arose with the Republican upsurge affecting troop movements. The first stages of the Easter uprising of 1916 gave promise of further problems. The NCC, being exclusively in the North, escaped any major disruption and James was able to keep matters running more or less normally.

The first major effect to have some bearing on the operation of the NCC was the relative importance of the Larne-Stranraer shipping route. As the main shipping connection with the UK, the Holyhead-Kingstown (Dun Laoghaire) run, was often curtailed by submarine activity and with the Heysham service suspended after the first year of the war, the Larne connection was, at times, the only means of travel across the Irish Sea.

Ireland never had conscription imposed, and so, initially, the drain on staff was relatively slight until, in October 1915, there was a general call for enlistment throughout the country. The railways immediately convened a meeting of all their Chairmen, at which it was decided that no member of staff should be called up without the company's permission, in order to avoid losing key people.

The war brought with it inflation. The costs and wages rose dramaticallyand in February 1915 James proposed to the Committee that war allowances be granted to counteract the effects of rising prices, in line with industrial practices.

Passenger services were cut back from 1st April, 1915, with a general increase in fares coming one year later.

Much of the engineering output of York Road works was diverted to wartime production, beginning in 1914 with the construction of 70 lorries for the War Office as part of the 5,000 to be built by railways throughout the UK. The following year production of 4½ inch shells began, and this continued for the duration.

James and his staff had much to do through the four years of war as shortages began to be felt. Initially, Baltic timber for sleepers became unavailable and sources closer to home had to be located. Brass and copper supplies were reserved for munitions work, meaning that steel boiler tubes had to be employed when replacements were needed. Rails were unobtainable, there being an embargo on their purchase and import, and track quality suffered considerably.

In 1914, as the war approached, Walter Bailey, the NCC accountant, was transferred to Derby. His place was taken by John Quirey, who had joined the B&NCR audit office in 1882 and had transferred to the accountant's office in 1891.

In 1917, Bailey died suddenly and Quirey moved to Derby to take his place. The vacancy at York Road was filled by William Valentine Wood, who had risen rapidly in the NCC accounts office since starting in a junior capacity in 1898. Wood's accountancy skills had him initially seconded to the Irish Railway Executive Committee at the recommendation of James Cowie. From there he was eventually recruited into the newly formed Ministry of Transport as director of finance. James was sorry to lose the solid backing of Wood in financial matters and certainly would not have realised then the even greater heights to which his accountant colleague was to advance.

The war and its after effects was to be the cause of a major downturn in railway prosperity throughout the United Kingdom. Four years of increased usage combined with the restrictions mentioned above were to cause extensive wear and tear on track and stock. Also, the wartime inflationary trends, coupled with Government restrictions on fare and goods rate increases, eroded profitability to such an extent that in 1919, with passenger and goods receipts being only some 75 per cent of pre-war levels, economies were necessary to counteract the net loss in revenue.

Some Governmental compensation was to come from the £3 million provided for Irish railways as a whole, £251,296 being set aside for the NCC. However, £124,990 had already been provided for various urgent needs, so just £126,306 remained to cover reparation from the effects of wartime working and economies - hardly a generous package. The pre-war profitability was never to return and James gloomily took stock of his railway's decline as his retirement approached.

For 1919, James was elected as Chairman of the Irish Railway Manager's Conference for a second time, his expertise being recognised yet again by this appointment. His workload thus remained at a high level and the intense pressure resulting from the wartime excesses must have turned his mind to thoughts of retirement (he was approaching 65). But his dedication to his task was to keep him in service for a few more years - until Grouping appeared on the horizon.

The supervisory body set up during the war, the Irish Railways Executive Committee, finally relinquished its powers on 31st December, 1919. James and the other managers still acted in an unofficial capacity as a standing committee whilst the newly created Ministry of Transport gradually took over the role previously held by the IREC. Much needed to be done in connection with the de-control of the railways and, additionally, the settlement of the compensation claims mentioned above. James' involvement was to organise the transfer of financial matters back to the control of the accounts department and prepare data to substantiate the claims pending. His rigid approach to these matters probably helped in dealing with the considerable red tape that must, of necessity, have ensued.

It was not until 15th August, 1921 that matters were fully back to normal and, as the NCC struggled to rectify a large backlog of maintenance tasks, the eight-hour working day for railwaymen was enforced in Ireland. The traffic department had, as a result of this, to employ an extra 27 per cent staff, and this at a time when costs had to be kept to a minimum was hardly helpful.

There was considerable industrial unrest which surfaced as peace returned, largely due to the threat of large lay-offs as industry changed course from wartime to peacetime production. James' earlier good relations with the employees was badly eroded when the York Road workers struck for three weeks in sympathy with the shipyard workers. The previous harmonious relationship between staff and employees seemed gone for ever.

B&NCR 0-6-0 No. 36 pilots a 2-4-0 on a lengthy goods train.

Bowman Malcolm, the Locomotive Superintendent of the B&NCR (NCC)   *Railway Magazine*

Chapter Thirteen

The Locomotives and Stock of the B&NCR

The role of General Manager encompasses the whole spectrum of running a service for the customers, of which the supply of suitable motive power and rolling stock is a vital ingredient. Such personages in those days implied by this narrative had the power to decide when and how many of the Locomotive Superintendent's designs or specifications for outside tender or construction at York Road works were to be supplied. The purse-strings of the capital equipment funds were at their behest. To complete the picture this account also covers the years up to Henry's retirement in 1931.

James Cowie and Bowman Malcolm, both Ulstermen, had for many years a close working relationship beginning when they were first employed by the Railway back in 1869. Once James had risen to be the Principal Assistant to Cotton in 1885 he would have been closely involved with Malcolm at a high level in any deliberations as to locomotive requirements.

Whilst Malcolm would have decided the final designs to be built, he would have done this in consultation with the Traffic Manager and General Manager and their immediate assistants. The York Road works of the B&NCR had, by the late 1880s, reached a stage where the complete construction and assembly of locomotives could be carried out. Indeed, as far back as 1870-73, three had been built there, albeit being largely extensive rebuilds of earlier types. For such a small concern, the ability to carry out complete manufacture showed that Cotton had placed it in a position where the necessary equipment could be purchased and installed so that limited production was feasible.

For the whole of James Cowie's career on the B&NCR the locomotive department was under the control of Bowman Malcolm, whom as we have seen, started his superintendency at the age of just 22. Early examples to come under Malcolm were all 2-4-0s built by Sharp, Stewart and Beyer, Peacock. All had been extensively rebuilt as the years went by and some 13 examples lasted until the early 1920s, notwithstanding their build dates of 1856 (Sharp, Stewart) and 1872 (Beyer, Peacock).

Malcolm began his design exercises in 1876 with a 2-4-0 express type, very similar in appearance to Ramsbottom's 'Newton' class on the LNWR. Three were built by Beyer, Peacock and all lasted well into the late-1930s, surely testimony of their robust design and reliability.

With the need to import coal supplies and the corresponding extra cost, it made sense for Malcolm to consider compound locomotives once the engineering aspects had been proved elsewhere. The economies in fuel consumption available by using compounding were well documented and so, in 1890, the first designs appeared on the B&NCR. A batch of 2-4-0s employing the Worsdell-von Borries two cylinder compound arrangement were built. They were significant on two counts, firstly, they were the first compounds to appear in Ireland and, secondly, they employed inside Walschaerts gear, the first locomotives to do so in the British Isles. The Irish 5 ft 3 in. gauge facilitated

0-6-0 No. 30, a pre-Malcolm design, but now (7th August, 1936) much rebuilt in service, seen here at Belfast.   *J.M. Jarvis Collection*

2-4-0 No. 27, a relic of the 1870s, much rebuilt and obviously reboilered still gong strong in September 1932.   *R.G. Jarvis/MRT*

the fitting of cylinders and valve gear neatly between the frames. Seven were built in total at Beyer, Peacock in Manchester. Two of this class achieved some distinction, firstly No. 57 when it was fitted with Ross pop safety valves, being the first locomotive in the world so fitted. The inventor of this valve, which was to be universally adopted as a standard component in the years that followed, lived in Coleraine and doubtless would have seen his invention in use on the locomotive as it passed through that town's station. No. 51, on the other hand was used for Malcolm's experiments into oil firing, being fitted with the Holden system as successfully used on the Great Eastern Railway in England. No evidence as to the outcome of these trials can be found, but this locomotive eventually reverted to normal coal firing.

The year 1892 saw the first 0-6-0 compounds, two being delivered for goods work. Again Beyer, Peacock, with whom Malcolm collaborated in the design stage, produced the pair, one of which, No. 54, lived on as a compound until the mid-1930s.

Further examples of passenger compounds appeared in 1895, with two 2-4-0s, Nos. 21 and 33. Then in 1897 five more 4-4-0s were built, these examples using the same motion and cylinders as the first batch of 2-4-0s their numbers being 51, 52, 65, 57 and 58.

Finally, in 1901, there appeared a batch of 4-4-0s, being the final development of the earlier types. Thirteen were built in total over seven years, the six examples, numbered 63-68, produced after 1905 coming from the Midland Railway plant at Derby.

Once the take-over by the Midland had taken place, future locomotive developments slowed down, as by 1908 the railway was adequately supplied with motive power. One of the surprising features of this take-over was the degree of autonomy given to the NCC, in particular as regards the liveries. Up until the MR bought out the B&NCR, the locomotives had been painted a light green, with red and white lining. This was changed at the end of 1903 to a dark olive green, again with red and white lining. Why this change was made is not known, but it was to last until after Grouping.

The compounds were not added to after this date, as by now superheating was in vogue and offering equivalent, if not better, economy. Malcolm accordingly set about designing an express 4-4-0 incorporating a superheated boiler. This appeared in 1914, a batch of two, numbered 69 & 70, being turned out by Derby works. They employed inside Walschaerts gear, as with all the compounds, and with a tractive effort of 17,390 lb. were, for some time, the most powerful express types on the NCC. Two more were built in 1922, Nos. 72 & 73, again at Derby, just before Malcolm retired.

The final offering to come from Malcolm's drawing board was a batch of three 0-6-0s employing the superheated boilers of the 1914 4-4-0s. Again these were simples, and were completed in March 1923, by Derby works, just after he retired. They were originally, in error, given the numbers 71 to 73, but these were allocated to the 4-4-0s. They entered service as X,Y and Z, before being allocated the numbers 13 to 15, previously used on some withdrawn locomotives. A summary of Malcolm's locomotive developments from 1890 to 1922 is to be found in *Table Eight* (page 137).

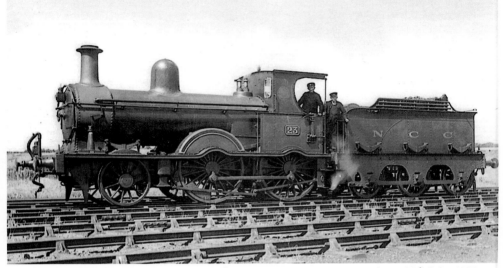

2-4-0 No. 23, Malcolm's first design for the B&NCR is found at Limavady on 30th July, 1935. Built by Beyer, Peacock in the 1870s the locomotive is little changed from the original.
R.G. Jarvis/MRT

0-4-0ST No. 16, one of two built for shunting work around York Road yard. The first appeared in 1874 and this one in 1914! *R.G. Jarvis/MRT*

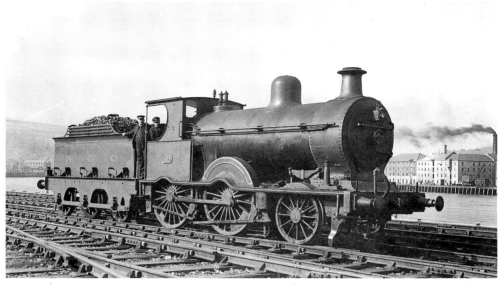

Another of Malcolm's first design, No. 46, as rebuilt with larger boiler, captured at Derry 15th May, 1937. *R.G. Jarvis/MRT*

2-4-0 No. 56 at York Road on 17th May, 1937. Still a compound, and substantially as built. *R.G. Jarvis/MRT*

Another long-term survivor as a compound, was 4-4-0 No. 55 *Parkmount* which had 7 ft diameter driving wheels, the largest in Ireland. Here it is caught at York Road on 17th May, 1937.
R.G. Jarvis/MRT

The other 7 ft 4-4-0, No. 50, as rebuilt to a simple and reboilered with an ex-MR unit in the mid-1920s.
R.G. Jarvis/MRT

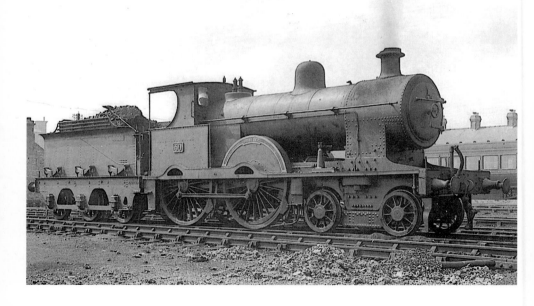

Table Eight

Locomotives designed and built for B&NCR during James Cowie's time

Date	Type	Cyls	Stroke	Pressure	Wheels	T.E.	No. built
				(Standard gauge)			
1876	2-4-0	17 in.	24 in.	n/a	6 ft 0 in.	-	3
1883	2-4-0T	15 in.	20 in.	n/a	5 ft 2 in.	-	4
1890	2-4-0	16 in. + 23¼ in.	24 in.	160 psi	6 ft 0 in.	11,600 lb.	7
1892	0-6-0	18 in. + 26 in.	24 in.	160 psi	5 ft 2 in.	16,920 lb.	2
1895	4-4-0	18 in. + 26 in.	24 in.	170 psi	7 ft 0 in.	13,380 lb.	2
1897	4-4-0	16 in. + 23½ in.	24 in.	160 psi	6 ft 0 in.	11,600 lb.	5
1901	4-4-0	18 in. + 26 in.	24 in.	175 psi	6 ft 0 in.	16,060 lb.	13
1914	0-4-0T	15 in.	20 in.	160 psi	4 ft 0 in.	12,750lb.	2
1914	4-4-0	19 in.	24 in.	170 psi	6 ft 0 in.	17,390 lb.	2
1922	4-4-0	19 in.	24 in.	170 psi	6 ft 0 in.	17390 lb.	2
			(Narrow Gauge)				
1892	2-4-2T	14 in. x 21 in.	20 in.	160 psi	3 ft 9 in.	13,150 lb.	6*

All the above locomotives were designed by Bowman Malcolm, the majority, up to 1901, being built by Beyer, Peacock. From 1890 all were compounds except the 1914 and 1922 batches.

There were also six Sharp, Stewart 2-4-0s built in 1856, plus nine Beyer, Peacock 2-4-0s of 1872 in addition to four classes of 0-6-0 totalling 14 in number (mainly Beyer, Peacock). All simples, and much rebuilt by the turn of the century.

Note: * Two in 1892 by Beyer, Peacock, with two more pairs in 1908-9 and 1919-20 from York Road works.

Thus by the early decades of the century, a high proportion of the locomotives in service were compounds, and were to remain in service as such for the remainder of Malcolm's career. Several had been built at the small York Road works following its expansion of manufacturing capability.

Although Bowman Malcolm is renowned for his narrow gauge tanks, so far as that type of locomotive is concerned on the standard gauge only two classes were to appear. In the early days of James and Henry Cowies' railway careers, tank locomotives were few in number. There were a few antiquated 2-2-2Ts from Fairbairn and Sharp, Stewart, one of which survived until 1906, but many had been withdrawn or rebuilt as 2-4-0 tender types by 1870. Not until 1882 did Malcolm produce a tank design, a 2-4-0T of which four were built by Beyer, Peacock in 1883. Useful little engines, they were occasionally found on Larne trains, but were employed primarily to take trains for Coleraine, Portrush or Londonderry to Greenisland where a main line locomotive would be put on at the reversal needed there. All these tanks were rebuilt as saddle tanks, two in 1891 and the others in 1911 and 1914. They lasted until the early 1930s when the construction of the Greenisland loop made their duties unecessary. One other tank design of Malcolm was the single 0-4-0T of class 'N', based on a design of 1876, of which one was still in service. This second example was constructed at York Road works in 1914 for shunting duties in the York Road yards, which it carried out until withdrawal in 1951.

Left: Works photograph of narrow gauge 2-4-2T No. 70.

Below: Narrow gauge 2-4-2T No. 111, of the original 1892 batch of two, prepared to leave Ballymena with a freight on 20th March, 1939.
R.G. Jarvis/MRT

No. 54, one of a pair built as compounds in 1892, is found still in service in 1937 at Derry.
R.G. Jarvis/MRT

As James retired, the three new superheated 0-6-0s ordered from Derby were delivered and entered service. Here No. 14 of that batch awaits further duties at York Road on 20th March, 1939. *R.G. Jarvis/MRT*

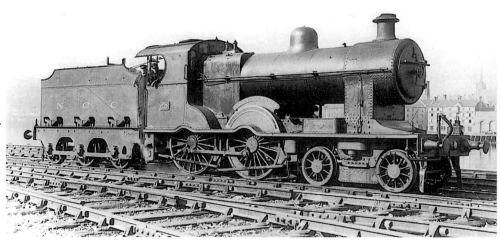

4-4-0 No. 28 *County Tyrone*, a rebuild of the 2-4-0 compound of class 'C'. The boiler is now a standard LMS 'G6' type, seen at Derry 15th May, 1937.   *R.G. Jarvis/MRT*

Formerly heavy compound No. 4, this simple rebuild is renumbered No. 62 and named *Slemish*. Here it is ready to depart from Larne in 1932.   *R.G. Jarvis/MRT*

The narrow gauge acquisitions of the B&NCR were, in the most part, rather run down when taken over, particularly in respect of the locomotive stock. Malcolm appraised the situation on these lines and, in 1892, designed a 2-4-2 tank locomotive for them. This was rather unique, being a compound design from the start, using the Worsdell-von Borries system, two being built initially by Beyer, Peacock. So successful were these, that four more were constructed at York Road, two in 1908-9 and two in 1919-20 to replace the older types still in service. The original need for these powerful tanks was to haul the boat expresses on the Ballymena to Larne line, which began shortly after this line commenced passenger services in 1888.

James would have been considerably involved in the managerial decisions surrounding the provision of the necessary funds to permit the production of all these locomotives, working closely with Malcolm.

All through the time of upgrading the locomotive part of York Road to permit complete locomotive construction, the carriage works had produced large numbers of carriages and wagons as they were needed, and continued to do so after the Midland take-over.

When Bowman Malcolm retired in 1922, he was succeeded by William K. Wallace in the dual civil and locomotive engineer role. Wallace had served in Malcolm's staff since 1906 and was regarded as a natural successor, being a first-class engineer, particularly in the civil engineering sphere. He quickly consolidated his promotion by establishing H.P. Stewart as his mechanical assistant and F.W. Crofts as the civil engineering assistant. Freeman Wills Crofts later became well-known as a writer of detective novels featuring Inspector French. He was in the employ of the NCC until 1929, when he resigned and took up writing full time.

The three 0-6-0s, Malcolm's final design, were finished off under Wallace, before he turned his mind to designing a new 4-4-0, based on the successful 1914 superheated type. Train weights were increasing, and extra, more powerful, locomotives were required. Ten of this design were authorised in 1924 and the LMS influence was to be found in the use of that line's class '2P' superheated boiler. It made economic sense to use this standard part, as well as boiler mountings and cab. Three of this batch were built at York Road, the remaining seven coming from the North British Locomotive Co. in Glasgow.

Prior to his retirement Malcolm had started to rebuild some of his compounds, two of the 'B' class light compounds having been dealt with in 1921. These incorporated larger boilers of 170 psi pressure. Wallace continued the rebuilding, but with one significant difference, the engines were changed to simples, using the class 'U' cylinders lined up to 18 inches. These, and all further rebuilds, were products of York Road works.

In 1926, the last example of the first batch of light compounds of class 'B', built in 1897, was converted to a simple using a spare boiler available. Also in this year two of the class 'C' light compound 2-4-0s were rebuilt as two-cylinder simple 4-4-0s.

For the remaining years of our narrative - up to 1931 - gradual rebuilding of most of the remaining light and heavy compounds continued, producing classes 'A1' and 'B3'. These compound to simple conversions had one further

The class 'U1' rebuild was an attractive locomotive, originally 2-4-0 No. 33 in James' days, No. 3 *Glenaan* is pictured at Ballymena on 20th March, 1939.   *J.M. Jarvis*

The small, high-pitched, boiler shows up well in this picture of the rebuilt former heavy compound No. 65 *Knockagh* at Belfast York Road Shed, 20th March, 1939.   *R.G. Jarvis/MRT*

unusual feature, they both employed interchangeable boilers having pressures of either 170 psi or 200 psi. This complicated matters so far as tractive effort was concerned. The above locomotive developments between 1922 and 1931 are summarised in *Table Nine*.

Table Nine

Locomotives designed and built for B&NCR after Grouping until Henry Cowie's retirement, 1923-1931

Date	Type	Cyls	Stroke	Pressure	Wheels	T.E.	No. built
				NEW			
1923	0-6-0	19 in.	24 in.	170 psi	5 ft 2 in.	20,030 lb.	3
1924	4-4-0	19 in.	24 in.	170 psi	6 ft 0 in.	17,390 lb.	10
				REBUILT			
1924	4-4-0	18 in.	24 in.	170 psi	6 ft 0 in.	15,610 lb.	2*
1926	4-4-0	18 in.	24 in.	170/200 psi	6 ft 0 in.	15,610/18,360 lb.	3*
1926	4-4-0	18 in.	24 in.	170/200 psi	6 ft 0 in.	15,610/183,60 lb.	2†
1926-31	4-4-0	18 in.	24 in.	170/200 psi	6 ft 0 in.	15,610/18,360 lb.	9#

Notes: * Rebuilt from light compound class 'B' (4-4-0)
         † Rebuilt from light compound class 'C' (2-4-0)
         # Rebuilt from heavy compound class 'A'. The balance of four of this class were similarly treated up to 1936.

By the time Henry Cowie retired, plans were afoot to increase the express fleet by planning for some six-coupled tender locomotives which were to materialise in a variant of the LMS Fowler 2-6-4T, but this modernisation is outside the scope this text. Both James and Henry probably were aware of this development and would certainly have approved of the introduction of really up-to-date types.

As with other railways, the early carriage stock of the B&NCR comprised four-wheeled compartment coaches, later augmented by six-wheel stock. Three classes were accommodated, and all of the new stock was built at York Road. During James Cowie's time, all carriages and wagons were designed and built under the superintendency of Bowman Malcolm who, as we shall see later, was very forward thinking in the introduction of new types of stock, particularly for goods use.

By 1882, in line with developments on other railways and to meet safety legislation then under consideration, the decision was made to fit all passenger stock with the automatic vacuum brake. This was a slow process, not being fully completed until 1893. However, this early adoption date made the B&NCR the first railway in Ireland to adopt an automatic system, which became compulsory all over the British Isles following the Armagh tragedy in 1889.

On 16th September, 1885, not long after James Cowie had been promoted to Assistant to the General Manager, the York Road carriage works were badly damaged by a fire. Several coaches being built and stock under repair were

The 'U2' conversion of the heavy compounds resulted in very much a 'Midlandised' engine both in fittings and style. No. 86, unnamed, prepares for service at York Road, 7th August, 1936.

J.M. Jarvis

No. 41, a 2-4-0 originally built by Beyer, Peacock in 1872 was not scrapped until 1933. Just before withdrawal it is found outside York Road Shed in September 1932.   *R.G. Jarvis/MRT*

destroyed. The insurance was adequate to cover the losses and rebuilding of the works that resulted. Production was resumed early the following year in the rebuilt premises and the temporary loss of stock did not appear to affect the running of the railway too much.

In 1888 a batch of new 6-wheel coaches was produced to augment the numbers available, for schedules were increasing as passenger traffic grew. York Road turned out the first bogie coach to run on the B&NCR in 1893. More followed, with some based on Swiss prototypes, being saloon types with a central corridor and railed and covered platforms at each end. These latter vehicles were usually found on the Larne boat trains and Portrush expresses. The loading gauge associated with the Irish 5 ft 3 in. gauge also permitted space for eight passengers to be seated in first class compartments.

By the mid-1890s the demand for more bogie stock was such that some batches had to be purchased from outside contractors, York Road being fully committed on other matters. Also, slip coaches made their appearance on the B&NCR being introduced to permit speeding up of some major expresses by eliminating stops at intermediate stations.

Catering facilities on trains first appeared in 1896 with the construction of two saloons having limited kitchen facilities. Three years later the first purpose-built dining car entered service, being initially rostered for the 12 noon Portrush express and evening return train. For 2s. one could choose from a lunch menu of lobster, cold veal and ox tongue, pressed beef, chicken and ham, pigeon and ham pies, or roast lamb and mint sauce. Dinner was 3s.

Tourism was a major source of income, particularly in the summer months, and often the B&NCR was called upon to produce special trains to accommodate this demand. The Northern Counties Hotel at Portrush thrived on these specials as well as the regular services.

One of the famous instances of regular specials hired for tours of Ulster produced the 'Holden' train in 1902. A.W. Holden was a hotel owner who regularly hired a train from the B&NCR for his summer tour programme , 'Holden's Popular Tour', using his hotel, the Laharna in Larne as a base. The tour visited Belfast, Portrush, the Giant's Causeway, Ballymoney, Ballycastle, Carrick-a-Rede, Parkmore and Glenariff, and Whitehead in six days. This constituted some 400 miles of train travel and 40 miles by road; all for the cost of £2 7s. 6d. So popular was this that it continued until World War I put a permanent end to it. The income from this, and other specials, was sufficient for James to authorise Malcolm to design a rake of coaches especially for such services. York Road accordingly turned out a special set comprising three saloon coaches and a dining saloon with kitchen, all first class. The resulting vehicles were very luxurious indeed, with match-boarding on the lower panels, and recessed Pullman style doors to the end vestibules. These features combined with the plush interior finish was a tribute to the craftsmen in the York Road works.

The years from 1896 to 1904 saw a 23 per cent growth in passenger traffic, and no less than 112 more coaches were added to the fleet, which now totalled 336, including the Holden stock. The population of Belfast had risen dramatically in the second half of the century, from 30,000 in 1850 to 360,000 in 1900. With the

"Holden's Tours." Laharna Hotel, Larne, Co. Antrim.

8-wheel dining saloon No. 13 in use on 'Holden's Tours'.   *John Alsop Collection*

Two of the three tram engines of the Portstewart Tramway are seen in storage in the York Road carriage shed on 17th May, 1937. One now resides in the Hull Transport Museum and the other is to be found in the Ulster Folk and Transport Museum.   *R.G. Jarvis/MRT*

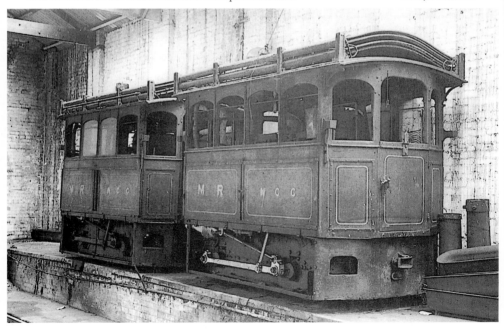

city bursting at the seams, many of the increased population elected to live out of the city. This provided a large commuter market which the railways promoted and absorbed eagerly, thus obtaining vastly increased passenger receipts. The increase in train capacity at York Road mentioned in Chapter Ten was a direct result of this growth.

Narrow gauge carriage stock totalled 33 examples at the peak of services on those lines, with some splendid bogie vestibuled carriages for the boat expresses on the Ballymena and Larne lines. These latter examples were designed and built at York Road by Bowman Malcolm, and were 50 ft in length and 8 ft wide.

The B&NCR and NCC were never to have large freight services. The majority of all large companies were in and around the Belfast area, so the transport of quantities of heavy loads across the province did not arise. The majority of freight services to the southern parts of Ireland were covered by the Great Northern. In 1903, at the Midland take-over, there were 2,294 goods vehicles of all types on the B&NCR, many of which were becoming worn out. In the early years of the NCC, up to 1912, a considerable number of new vehicles were produced, 190 covered vans and 50 open wagons for the broad gauge alone. Some 300 of the stock that existed before 1908 were unbraked and, when the Board of Trade regulations came in requiring all freight stock to have a basic hand operated braking system, these were progressively fitted to the offending vehicles.

Despite the small amount of freight work on the railway, by 1902 there were some very advanced vehicles in service. Malcolm had introduced some 30 ton bogie wagons for large loads. There were also some refrigerator vans in use and, for bulk carriage of coal or ballast either 6-wheel 16 ton or 4-wheeled 20 ton wagons.

The narrow gauge branches were not forgotten, with 38 eight ton side tipping wagons being built in 1906 to replace some older, unstable, 4 ton versions. In 1907 came a big contract for the transport of iron ore from the mines near Parkmore on the former Cushendall railway to Larne harbour for export. This amounted to some 35,000 tons per year, and resulted in the provision of 100 new wagons and the 1908 pair of compound tanks to cope with the demand, which hitherto had been met by road transport.

All these authorisations for new stock would have passed through James' hands as the NCC continued in its profitable years before the war came to upset finances. The Midland was very content to let matters run in James' and Malcolm's capable hands and take the steady income that the updating and growth of the railway produced.

To implement the design tasks surrounding all the railway's needs for locomotive and stock, Bowman Malcolm had charge over a team of just 10 key technical staff, five covering locomotive work and five on carriages and wagons. The York Road works staff totalled around 350 for all disciplines. His civil engineering department was even more numerous, with 14 key technical staff plus 670 others to cover the permanent way and works areas. The sum total to come under Malcolm was nearly 48 per cent of the total workforce on the railway. The fact that he managed all this competently for over a decade amplifies his exceptional managerial skills.

B&NCR 0-6-0 class 'E' compound No. 53.

B&NCR 'Jubilee' 4-4-0 No. 50 is seen leaving Ballymena with a passenger train.

Chapter Fourteen

The Post-War Years and Retirement for James: 1919-1923

The political situation in Ireland resulting from the Easter 1916 uprising was, by the end of World War I, moving relentlessly towards the break away of what was to be the Irish Free State and then the Republic from the United Kingdom. The strongly Protestant North was, however, determined to remain within the United Kingdom, and had no wish to enter into home rule. The railway companies, recovering from the excesses of the war, were likely to be affected in some way by the outcome of the delicate political negotiations, with those having facilities in both North and South worrying about any split in territorial choices. The NCC, however, was totally contained in what was to become Northern Ireland and, as such, little affected by the changes.

Also around this time, Henry's daughter, Mabel Sarah, known as Sally, having completed her education at Methodist College, Belfast, which she had attended since 1913, obtained a place at Queen's University. Here she intended to read English, a subject in which she had won prizes during her school-days, with the ultimate goal of entering the teaching profession. Henry and Margaret were justly proud of her progress.

Although James had relatively little involvement with the CDRJC narrow gauge concern, he would have given tacit approval to the cost cutting moves of that line's General Manager, Henry Forbes, in his attempts to return that concern to profitability. This, indeed, was eventually achieved mainly by some pioneering introductions of diesel powered railcars. A man not to be trifled with, Forbes proved his worth one day in 1920 when a CDRJC train, on which he was travelling, was held up at gunpoint near Dunbar. The manager grabbed a revolver kept nearby, jumped down and ran along to the engine where the raiders were. A brief fusilade of shots then took place, without any injuries on either side, before the raiders decided that it would be safer to retire, and took off. Forbes, however, was not content with this and chased after the culprits. One of them was obviously not much of an athelete, for he was captured and taken to the nearest police station to be arrested and charged.

Just as James was preparing for his retirement, a limited amount of trouble arose on the NCC lines, which ran primarily through Loyalist territory, in 1921-22, emanating from the then on-going civil strife as Ireland moved towards partition. Several cases of arson and malicious damage occurred, mainly directed at stations, signal boxes and the telegraph lines. Both James and Henry were much engaged in assessing the reports on damage caused and preparing compensation claims, in addition to seeing to the speedy restoration of disrupted services.

The only major attempt on the track itself was on 19th May, 1922, when a bridge between Killegar and Dunloy, on the main line to Ballymoney, was damaged by an explosive device. Trains were, as a result, unable to use this bridge for four days whilst repairs were carried out. The conditions surrounding these 'troubles' had a serious effect on the railway revenue, in that the curfew enforced in Belfast from 1920 to 1924 affected services adversely.

Henry's daughter, Sally, who was to become a teacher following her Queen's University studies.
Anne Parkhill

As retirement drew nearer for James, his workload grew due to the post-war maintenance arrears. The troubles added to his worries and it must have been with some relief that he tendered his resignation in August 1922.

Some of the other railways were not so lucky, with those in the South badly affected by the ensuing Civil War as opposing factions fought over whether or not to accept the Treaty. Considerable damage was done to stock and track facilities until hostilities were finally brought to a halt in 1923.

But this is taking us too far ahead. To return to the immediate post-war years the NCC was feeling the effects of road transport competition. This was caused by the large number of common carrier services offered by the multitude of small concerns being set up using cheap Army surplus lorries then becoming available. As the year progressed, this competition, not hampered by the restrictions still in force on the railways, became serious and James ordered that a survey be made into the effects of this on the goods traffic. The conclusions of the ensuing report showed that a staggering 50,000 tons of goods traffic alone was being lost each year. As the Governmental control on the railways was relaxed, it became possible to reduce the rates for both goods and passenger traffic by some 25 per cent and regain some of the losses.

Perhaps the full impact of this post-war competition can be better emphasised by comparing the 1913 and 1922 results for passenger and goods traffic on the NCC:

	1913	*1922*
Passengers	3,857,000	2,825,062
Goods traffic	897,777 tons	675,017 tons

One particular event, which had been in the planning stage for some time now, and actually transcended the time over which James handed over control to his successor, was the planning and building of the new Bann bridge at Coleraine. Originally planned in 1914, and delayed by the war, matters recommenced in 1919 with the purchase of the land necessary for the re-routing of the line. Malcolm, in his guise of civil engineer, designed the structure of the new bridge, employing the Strauss underhung bascule principle for the opening portion, the first time this method had been used in the UK. The contract for the structure was put out for tender, and the quote of Sir A.G. Armstrong, Whitworth & Co. Ltd, for £62,500 was accepted. In early 1921, work began on the new track alignment and bridge piers, but it was not until 21st March, 1924 that the bridge was opened to traffic. Bowman Malcolm, although retired, was in the inspection party prior to the opening, but James, also retired, was not present.

Across the Irish Sea, from 1st January, 1923, the railways in the remainder of the British Isles were in the throes of being completely reorganised in the Grouping that followed the relinquishing of Government controls. The Midland was to become part of the London Midland & Scottish Railway, this new amalgam taking the NCC under its wing.

As James prepared for retirement his successor was being selected, initially thought to be Robert Darragh, recently promoted to Traffic Superintendent. However, events in England were to dictate otherwise, as the Midland placed its man, James Pepper, in charge. Darragh was given the position of Principal Assistant.

James Pepper, who took over as General Manager
of the NCC from James Cowie.
Railway Magazine

W.K.Wallace, who replaced Bowman Malcolm and
was, in later years, to become the Chief Civil
Engineer of the LMS.   *Railway Magazine*

The effects of the war on industrial practices and finances had swept away the old Victorian management principles upon which the railways had been built. Now it was time for the more radical modern management methods to take over and translate the railway industry into the faster moving environment of the 1920s and 1930s. James Cowie was an excellent manager whilst the older principles lasted, but he must have sensed the changes in the air and this probably motivated him to consider retirement earlier than he might otherwise have planned. His strict and formal outlook on matters would have led to an inflexible approach and some friction as new practices were adopted. He and Adelaide were well-established in their comfortable house 'Lancetta' on the then fashionable Antrim Road, Henry was living nearby at Carrickfergus, and Robert up to now was still abroad in Europe, and seemed to be settled in Italy for some time.

James had adopted Edward Cotton's principle of regular monthly reporting by each department to the Board. This rather Victorian approach not only produced vast amounts of paperwork, but also missed out on one vital ingredient, this being the cross-referencing of matters such that the individual reports could be easily collated. The Board members were obviously expected to be capable of achieving this, and probably did, at the expenditure of considerable study and time.

Clearly, with management styles changing, this form of reporting had to change and so it fell to James' successor to introduce a new system whereby the reports went to the General Manager. The latter, with his staff, then collated them into a single comprehensive report in which all important statistics were accurately presented. This method also meant that the Manager had at his finger-tips the latest information on the many features making up the running of the railway.

Henry continued in the service of the NCC. Amongst his many attributes he had a great sense of humour and always enjoyed the company of others. Although trained under James' attitudes and outlook, his ability to see the funny side of things broadened his outlook and clearly assisted his fitting into the new order which the LMS introduced. One only has to look at a photograph of James and Henry to see the difference in their personalities.

James finally retired in 1922. Aged 67, he had spent some 53 years in the service of the railway. He was granted a pension of £1,000 (half his final salary). Also retiring at the same time was Bowman Malcolm, one of the longest serving Locomotive Superintendents of all time. Their chosen date was 30th September, of that year, and thus they escaped the inevitable management upsets caused by the Grouping.

A few weeks after his retirement, James Cowie was, on the 16th November, presented with a token of esteem from the railway and shipping companies gathered at the Railway Managers Conference in Dublin. The venue was, as usual, the Irish Railway Clearing House. The current Chairman of the Conference, Mr E.A. Neale, presided and placed on record the members' appreciation of the valuable help which James had, at all times, given to the Conference during his membership. He spoke of their regret at the loss of James' experience and judgment in their many deliberations. Walter Baird, of the Burns and Laird Lines, spoke on behalf of all the shipping companies and confirmed all that Mr Neale had said.

James Cowie at retirement.

Anne Parkhill

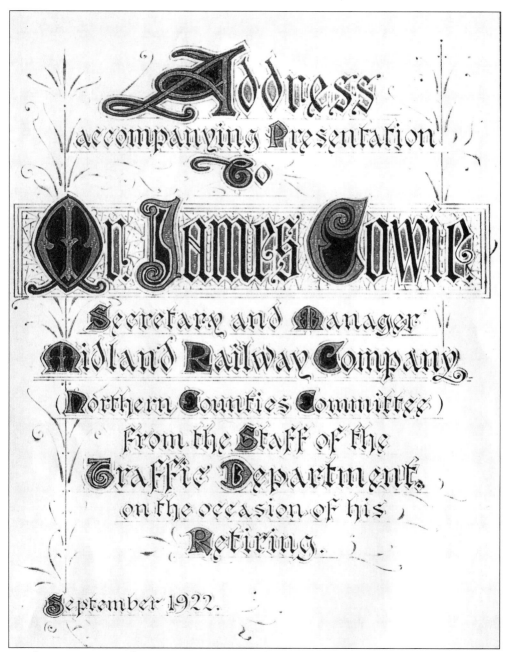

The opening page of the book given to James on the occasion of his retirement.   *Anne Parkhill*

To wind up the speeches, Mr Hunt, representing the smaller Irish railways and Mr Ingram of the Transport Department, Ministry of Industry and Commerce, paid tribute to the many good qualities possessed by Mr Cowie.

James suitably replied to these eulogies praising his managerial style and bade farewell to the many colleagues with whom he had dealt over the years. Following this, a gift comprising an ivory-mounted fitted gentleman's suitcase was made to him on behalf of all present.

More presentations were made at the end of November at a joint farewell gathering for Cowie and Malcolm held at the Station Hotel, Belfast. The Directors, officers, and Head Office staff of the company were present to see James receive a solid silver tray and his wife a diamond pendant.

Mr Charles Booth, representing the directorate, made a speech praising both Cowie's and Malcolm's devotion to their duties for the NCC, mentioning especially their consideration to all with whom they came into contact. Further speeches amplified the comments made by Booth.

James expressed his thanks on behalf of his wife and himself, stating that the gifts received would be a reminder of the appreciation of the donors. Following the management presentation the staff of the Traffic Department presented Cowie with a solid silver tea service, whilst Mrs Cowie received a silver trinket box. This was accompanied by a leather bound album containing an illuminated Address and specially commissioned pictures by J.W. Carey, of York Road Terminus, Belfast referred to in Chapter Ten. The album also included the names of all the subscribers.

The words of the Address dated September 1922 clearly indicate the esteem in which James Cowie was held by his employees:

Dear Sir,

After a period of over fifty years spent amongst us, we cannot allow you to leave the scene of your labours without an expression of our deep regret at your departure, and of our great admiration of your many excellent qualities of heart and mind.

Beginning at the bottom of the ladder in the Managerial Department, you rose step by step, until by your energy, judgement and conspicuous ability, you became the head of one of the most successful railway undertakings in Ireland.

Your sterling character and kindly consideration of every member of your staff, won for you their profound regard, and ensured at all times their cordial co-operation in your efforts to advance the interests of the Company, which you so ably served. It is our fervent wish that you may live long to enjoy your well earned leisure, which we sincerely hope may be made happy by every blessing that Heaven can bestow.

And so ended an illustrious career on the railways in the North of Ireland. James lived on quietly in retirement at his Antrim Road home, which is today part of a medical centre covering North Belfast and Newtownabbey.

Without the expert guidance of James Cowie and his team at York Road headquarters, the NCC would not have the accolades it received for the first two decades of the 20th century. Against the backdrop of wartime restrictions, economic depression and road transport competition the railway offered a reliable and economic means of transport between the principal cities in the North of Ireland and throughout much of the Province. The foundation of wise management laid by Cotton, Cowie and their assistants ensured that the

Midland Railway (and, subsequently, the LMS) received a good return on the 1903 investment.

One of James' first decisions following the return to normal after the war and his retirement was to visit his brother Robert, now settled in Italy. Henry, who also had not seen Robert for some time, also indicated his intention to visit their itinerant brother. And so they set off together, with their wives, for Rome in 1923, for a family reunion. One result of this trip was that day spent at Rome railway station as recounted in Chapter Eight.

By the end of 1923, just following James' retirement, the Ballycastle Railway's financial problems finally came to a point where the combined total of working losses and debit balance of the share account reached the sum of £7,271 on the year. Cotton's unofficial advisory capacity, mentioned in Chapter Nine, had turned the Ballycastle into a profitable concern, but following his death in 1899 matters had been neglected. Therefore a slow but steady decline had set in and, accelerated by the effects of the wartime inflationary pressures, had reached crisis point. The situation was desperate and on 17th January, 1924 the Ballycastle Board asked the NCC to purchase the line. Having initially received no reply, the decision to close the line was taken at a Board meeting one week later. The shareholders agreed to this by the 8th February and after 24th March the services were suspended.

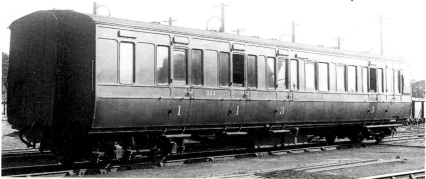

Narrow gauge bogie carriage No. 353. *John Alsop Collection*

Narrow gauge bogie carriage No. 352 at Ballycastle on 8th July, 1936. *John Alsop Collection*

Further representation to the NCC produced an offer of £10,000 for the complete railway. In early April the shareholders asked for this to be increased, and increased it was - to £12,500! Following a Special General Meeting on 4th May the sale was authorised and the NCC took over, its first priority to rectify the line's very run-down condition. This took many weeks and not until 11th August was the line considered suitable to be reopened. As with all take-overs of this kind, an Act of Parliament was required to seal the merger. Accordingly, the LMS (Ballycastle Railway Vesting) Act was raised, being the first railway Act to be passed by the recently formed Northern Ireland Parliament.

Henry Cowie, never quite as gifted as brother James, nevertheless had made his way up the ladder to the not insubstantial post of chief clerk, ably supporting his brother in the latter years of his General Managership. Many of the decisions affecting the running of the railway would have passed through their hands to the Committee for ratification and action. Whilst James retired some three months before Grouping, Henry, being some 16 years his junior, worked on in his post to see the NCC transformed into a more recognisable arm of the LMS and, in fact, became the last management link with the old B&NCR.

Not long after the Grouping had taken place, Henry was delighted at his daughter Mabel Sarah's award of a First Class Honours degree in English from Queen's. Shortly after this she embarked on her teaching career, initially obtaining a post at Ashleigh House School in Belfast and then teaching in India before becoming Principal of Neville's Cross Teachers' Training College in Durham.

The remainder of this narrative will be concerned with the happenings on the NCC, for the rest of Henry's career, as the whole railway spectrum in the United Kingdom altered. The Derby design centre of the LMS was also to become more dominant in matters concerning new locomotives and stock.

No. 101, one of six 2-4-2Ts of Bowman Malcolm, awaits departure from Ballycastle on 29th July, 1935, having been transferred from the Ballymena and Larne to Ballycastle Railway.
J.M. Jarvis

Chapter Fifteen

Grouping, and into the Thirties with Henry: 1923-1931

We have seen that the Midland influence on the B&NCR (NCC) in the early days after the take-over was relatively minimal as regards the running of the railway, and also in respect of locomotive and carriage stock, even down to the liveries. Whilst the Derby works of the MR had assisted in the production of a few locomotives, no major effort had been made to implant the ideas of the Derby design staff on Malcolm and his technical office. The MR obviously recognised an efficient concern and, for the first 19 years of the alliance, other than controlling the purse-strings, played little part in the day-to-day management of locomotive or stock design.

Once Grouping was assured, the new conglomerate of the LMS proceeded to stamp its authority on the NCC. Now that James Cowie and Bowman Malcolm had both retired, the way was open for their own people to be implanted with the minimum of disruption and upset. Accordingly, James Cowie had handed over his responsibilities to James Pepper who had, prior to this, been the Assistant Goods Manager of the Midland Railway, based at Derby.

Pepper had a little over three months to settle in at York Road before the formation of the LMS. Matters ran much as before, the only tangible evidence of any influence from Euston being the gradual introduction of the LMS style maroon livery.

Although policy dictated that all new locomotives for the NCC were eventually to be the responsibility of the Derby works, the first examples to be produced for Northern Irish use were to be the 10 examples based on Malcolm's last 4-4-0 design. Of these, three were built at York Road and seven by the North British Locomotive Company. These did however employ certain Derby features - boilers, cabs, tenders, styling, amongst others, as mentioned in the chapter on locomotive developments. It made technical sense to utilise many standard parts then in production for LMS types.

With James now retired, Henry continued in his position of chief clerk in the Manager's office. His extensive experience, coupled with the fact that the LMS was content to continue the system of control adopted by the NCC, made certain that his position was assured. As in the 1903 take-over there were no changes at the top and no sudden policy alterations until, in February 1924, the minutes make the comment, 'the future colours of the Committee's engines shall be the LM&SR Co's Standard Lake'.

Also discussed at this meeting was the state of the passenger rolling stock, much of which was obsolescent, the newest examples dating from 1906. Accordingly, 24 new carriages were ordered so that adequate modern stock was available for the principal trains. The LMS influence was increased by the fact that these new additions were standard Derby products on 5 ft 3 in. gauge bogies.

One of the problems in these immediate post-war years was the huge increase in the wages bill and the implementation of the 8-hour working day, plus the

The new Bann bridge, opened in 1924. It was designed under Bowman Malcolm who at the end of his career also covered Civil Engineering matters.

John Alsop Collection and Railway Magazine

huge increase in road transportation competition. Passenger and freight levels then current presented falls of 27 per cent and 25 per cent respectively, compared to the pre-war figures. The operating ratios were 68 per cent for pre-war and 91 per cent for post-war respectively. So, clearly, economies needed to be made.

In 1924 the Manager's office was busy organising the initial economies proposed, which included reducing station staffs drastically and downgrading many of the smaller stations to unstaffed halts. One particular item of essential capital expenditure involved the track and signalling at York Road, the former being completely renewed and the latter replaced by colour light signals, the first to appear in Ireland and, indeed, one of the largest such applications so far in the British Isles. These were planned by Wallace, the Chief Engineer, and installed in conjunction with an extensive track circuiting system and route indicators. Operation of the new system was from a signal cabin, built between the main running lines and the goods yard to contain the operating system. The electricity required was obtained from the Belfast Corporation system, and a petrol generating set provided for use in case this external supply failed.

As the 1920s progressed, all the railways in Ireland were in deep financial trouble and it was noticeable on the NCC that the previously good industrial relations had soured to the point that strikes began to occur. That the railway's financial straits were in a perilous state did not seem to worry the workforce was doubly annoying to the management of the day. In 1923 York Road works was brought to a virtual standstill by a strike of 120 shopmen, asking for better bonus payments. This dispute lasted six weeks before arbitration resolved it, to the benefit of the NCC. James, from his retirement home, would have been greatly saddened by this breakdown in the good relationship with the workforce which he had carefully nurtured.

In November 1923 all the Irish railways, both North and South, proposed a cut in wages of all grades except enginemen of 4s. 7d. per week. The NCC wages bill would have been reduced by £15,455 a year. Simultaneously the companies wanted the eight-hour day ruling abolished.

Following these proposals, the Irish Railway Wages Board, which covered both the railway companies and trades unions on both sides of the border, was formed. Throughout the 1920s this unique body of cross-border co-operation did its best to cut back on wages in an attempt to rectify the dire financial straits of the Irish railways. This body was, however, unable to effect any turnaround in the companies' fortunes, largely due to the demoralising impact of wage cuts coupled with the onset of the depression. Considerable trouble lay ahead and Henry's normal cheerful approach to life must have been severely dented in his final years of office as he witnessed the crumbling of a once profitable railway into almost perpetual decline. Most certainly his decision to take early retirement was influenced by this.

The Northern Counties Hotel had, for many years, shuttled its clients to and from the station at Portrush by horse-bus. Somehow the updating of this somewhat obsolescent mode of transport got overlooked until 1925. How it survived for so long is a mystery, particularly as the Giant's Causeway Tramway had shown the potential of modern electric trams as far back as 1883, and also considering the NCC's involvement in supplementary bus services. Perhaps the relatively short journey involved from station to hotel did not warrant much capital expenditure on the mode of transport. Quite possibly Henry would have seen the amusing side of such an antiquated arrangement, with passengers stepping from the modern rolling stock to the decidedly Victorian horse-bus for the final haul to their luxury holiday abode.

The General Strike of 1926 affected the NCC's coal supplies, and passenger train mileage was forced down to 57 per cent of normal. Henry and his colleagues were busy organising the use of such coal supplies as were in stock to permit the limited services to be maintained for as long as possible.

One of the features of the NCC, encouraged by James, had been the investment in limited road transport to assist passengers and goods transfers in areas where there was no branch line. In particular James' introduction of bus services had proved successful, and so it was natural to consider expanding this when a large number of independent bus operators appeared in the 1920s. By October 1929 the NCC had some 22 buses in service. This, however, was just a beginning, as by April 1930 there were 84 buses, which rose to 118 by March 1931, just before Henry retired. This large investment necessitated the provision of space in the York Road works to cater for the major servicing needs of these vehicles, which had by now replaced some of the branch lines and narrow gauge passenger services. This permitted a reduction in locomotive numbers to effect a small reduction in running costs.

With the bus services doing well and being increased in frequency, a new central bus station was built by the NCC on the former premises of the New Smithfield Weaving Company. The total cost of this development, including the alterations to the building, came to £34,000. Smithfield bus station opened on 1st November, 1930.

Considerable reorganisation of all the bus services then took place, concentrating on the need to complement the train services and reducing the mileage on duplicated or competitive routes. The NCC was now the second largest bus operator in Northern Ireland, surpassed only by the Belfast Omnibus Company, and then only by a small number of vehicles owned by that concern.

As the 1920s progressed, W.V. Woods, James' old accountancy colleague, returned to railway service from the Ministry of Transport as director of transport accounting for the LMS, which put him into contact with those of his early days left in the York Road offices of the NCC. Henry would have felt proud of his earlier association with Woods, who rose to Vice-President of the LMS in 1929, replacing Quirey, also a York Road product. So, in the short space of seven years from Grouping this top position on the LMS had been held by products of York Road. This was by no means the end of the road for Woods, as he was eventually to be knighted in 1937, followed by the Presidency of the LMS after the untimely death of Lord Stamp in 1941. Yet another product of the Irish railways had proved to be a fine administrator. York Road had certainly proved to be a good training ground under the strict, but meticulous, managership of James Cowie.

One major civil engineering project which had been repeatedly brought up over the years concerned the construction of a loop line to eliminate the reversal of Portrush and Londonderry line trains at Greenisland, the connection from the Belfast-Larne line leading from the Larne direction. Not only did this reversal add time to the schedules, it also entailed the extra expense of providing a second engine for the first part of the journey from Belfast to Greenisland and vice versa, and with nearly half the trains involved in this manoeuvre, the potential saving was considerable.

Several proposals to eliminate this by track realignment and a loop had been mooted during James Cowie's General Managership, as far back as the 1890s, when one of the earliest proposals considered a tunnel through the Cavehill mountain, which lies at the north-eastern corner of Belfast on the northern shore of Belfast Lough. The first few miles of the railway ran around the base of this mountain on leaving York Road. The estimates for such an undertaking were, to say the least, considerable and could not be justified. By the late 1890s, further consideration of this large engineering project was being raised at Board meetings, but any decision to undertake it was shelved. The take-over of the B&NCR by the Midland in 1903, overshadowed any further plans for the tunnel and it was not until the early 1930s that the Greenisland reversal was eliminated - and then by a totally different means.

It fell to the latter years of Henry's time with the NCC for a firm plan to be made, under Pepper, to construct the loop. Planning started in 1927 when it was realised that Government aid would be available from the scheme to alleviate high levels of unemployment prevalent due to the current depression. The estimated cost was £200,000 of which half would be the associated labour costs. The Government unemployment relief assistance would cover three-quarters of the labour costs, the remainder being supplied by the LMS.

Planning went ahead and Henry was busily engaged organising some of this. The necessary Act was passed in Westminster on 4th June, 1928. Work, however, did not start in earnest until 1st January, 1931, just before Henry retired, delayed by economic uncertainties of the time with the depression that, by this time, was affecting the whole of the UK.

However, once matters were under way, up to 500 men were employed as direct labour, the railway preferring not to contract out the job. The large numbers employed certainly helped the unemployment situation in that part of Ulster quite markedly. The work was completed early in 1934.

By 1931, James had been retired eight years, living in the Antrim Road house, when Adelaide died. Henry and Margaret were still living at Carrickfergus and were able to offer support and comfort in the difficult early days of James' loss of his wife of 44 years. Sometime shortly after Adelaide died, James' sister Mary Parkhill, who had been widowed since 1913, and since then living in Chichester Road, Belfast, moved into the house to look after him. James needed a woman's guidance in domestic affairs. By this time three of Mary's four children were either married or away from home. Had any young children been around, this move would probably not have taken place, for James had difficulty in getting on with them, preferring to retire to another room if any visited, leaving instructions that there must be no noise. Mary's eldest daughter, Edith, who never married, came with her mother to assist in the running of affairs.

Above: James and Henry in retirement.   *Anne Parkhill*

Top right: James Cowie's 80th birthday was a time for the family to congregate. Here they record the event at 'Lancetta'. Henry is thought to have taken this photograph, hence his non-appearance.   *Anne Parkhill*

Right: In keeping with their close family ties, the Cowies and Parkhills gathered together on many occasions. This photograph was taken to record one such event. *Back row, left to right:* Revd James Parkhill, James Cowie, Robert (Bertie) Parkhill, Robert (Bobby) Parkhill, Henry Cowie. *Front row, left to right:* Adelaide Cowie, Mary Parkhill (née Coey), ?, Margaret Cowie (née Knox), Catherine Parkhill (née Coey).   *Anne Parkhill*

Far right: Henry and Margaret at yet another family gathering. A last photographic record.
          Anne Parkhill

Lancetta,

Antrim Road,

Belfast.

Mr R. G. Parkhill and Mrs J. W. Parkhill return sincere thanks for your very kind expressions of sympathy on the death of their brother, Mr James Cowie.

May, 1937.

The letter sent out from 'Lancetta' to acknowledge expressions of sympathy after James' death.
Anne Parkhill

The pressures of running the NCC throughout these traumatic years had their effects on all in management. By 1930, James Pepper, James Cowie's successor, was so run down by the General Manager's and Secretary's responsibilities that he asked for retirement on health grounds. Henry, in his responsible post of chief clerk had also suffered considerably and, as his 60th birthday approached, began to think about early retirement. All the earlier top people had now gone and Henry was virtually the last link, certainly the highest ranking official, with the original NCC as part of the Midland Railway. The working practices he had been brought up with had disappeared, the older Victorian values of rigid discipline and strict hierarchy having been replaced by the more flexible 20th century approach to management. He must have sensed that a new broom was needed to sort out the financial problems pressing on the railways everywhere in the UK and Ireland. It was time to bow out of the proceedings. He accordingly resigned in 1931 and settled back with Margaret to enjoy the years left to him.

Shortly before Henry retired, the NCC was planning a further trial of a railcar on lightly used services. The primary aim was to reduce running costs associated with the lengthy preparation and disposal times needed by steam locomotives. A vehicle which could be put into service at the touch of a button was needed, and provided, in the form of one powered by internal combustion engines. The design which emerged was powered by two 130 hp Leyland petrol engines and was built the year following Henry's retirement. This railcar, No. 1, was immediately successful, leading to further examples later that decade, and actually preceded the GWR entry into that form of transport, so often regarded as the pioneer in this respect on the UK railways.

August 1934 brought the death of Robert in Harrogate at the age of 83. James and Henry mourned the loss of their elder brother, James in particular, as he was the closest in years to Robert. Henry saw his eldest brother as a rather distant figure as, in his early years, Robert was already away from home studying at University prior to his return to Dublin and subsequent advancement.

Two years later, in February 1936 at the age of just 65, Henry passed away in Belfast. This early death was the result of illness brought on from injuries following a bad fall experienced whilst boarding a tram in Belfast. What exactly the injuries were is not clear, but they were severe enough to upset his health. His cheerful outgoing disposition was greatly missed by the family. In May 1937 Henry was joined by 81-year-old James. Both are buried at the City Cemetery, Belfast, as are their wives. Notably, Henry's grave is marked as Coey, James' grave having the Cowie spelling chosen by him all those years ago, although Henry's wife Margaret, who died in 1941, is recorded with the Cowie spelling.

Shortly before Henry's untimely death, the two brothers remaining in Belfast attended the funeral of their brother-in-law, the Revd James Parkhill, who died suddenly at home on 2nd February, 1935. They comforted their sister Catherine on her loss of this stalwart member of the Methodist Church with a long record of service throughout many circuits in Ireland, who had also been President of the Methodist Church in Ireland in 1923.

'Lancetta', James and Adelaide Cowie's last home. It still stands having been converted from this original state into a Medical Centre.   *Anne Parkhill*

Mary Parkhill continued living at 'Lancetta' the Antrim Road house for a short time after James' death, a short distance from her sister Catherine Parkhill (Mary and Catherine had married two brothers). The two sisters were kept busy answering the many letters from people who offered their condolences. A copy of the printed letter sent out by them is illustrated on page 166.

So ended the lives of three brothers who all chose the railways as a career. The spanned the years from those halcyon days when the train was King of Transportation over land, to the inter-war years as this mode of travel struggled to meet the competitive onslaught of the internal combustion engine on the roads.

Their respective skills in handling the complex tasks involved in engineering and management had helped to carry the Irish railways from the 19th to 20th centuries as a prime means of opening up that country to the new modern age, changing traditions and bringing new levels of prosperity to the population.

The real legacy left to the British railway scene by such as the Coey engineering and Cowie management expertise was to be experienced by the arrival on the railways in England of R.E.L. Maunsell and W.V. Woods respectively. The skills of these two examples of Irish training and background served with distinction on the British side of the Irish Sea to the benefit of the railways they joined.

Appendix

The 4-4-0 developments of R.E.L. Maunsell in relation to those of Robert Coey

Introduction

To analyse fully the 4-4-0 developments of R.E.L. Maunsell it is necessary to go back to his days under Robert Coey at the Inchicore works of the GS&WR, when that type of locomotive was the mainstay of express services on that railway, and indeed on many of the other railways in the British Isles. The Coey 4-4-0 is considered here as a baseline design from which he began his developments.

Experimental data on the performance of Coey locomotives is a rarity these days, with nearly a century having passed since testing was carried out. However, *The Engineer* for 8th November, 1905 contains an article describing the Marshall valve gear experiments on a class '305' 4-4-0, No. 307, which were carried out in July 1904. In that article there are a series of indicator diagrams, with relevant pressures and ihp's. These permit the analysis of the performance to a reasonable degree, the results of which suggest a maximum power output of 862 ihp at 52.5 mph, quite a commendable performance for a medium sized 4-4-0 in those days, see *Figure One*.

Exactly how much the freer exhaust permitted by the Marshall gear contributed to this power output is difficult to quantify without access to results from an unmodified locomotive. These latter results were obtained for comparison at the time, but no diagrams for the unmodified locomotive have survived, save for a plot of the relative speeds achieved by the modified and unmodified engines with similar train loads. The clear advantage of a freer exhaust, permitting faster running and better hill climbing due to reduced back pressure, is evident in the plot of speeds to be found in the article in question.

The values of ihp obtained from the data available shows that Robert Coey certainly developed his moderately sized 4-4-0s into some powerful examples of motive power, especially when one takes into consideration the boiler pressure and cylinder size, both slightly less than many contemporary types on the mainland. The Inchicore design team were certainly capable of producing a locomotive many of the railways in Great Britain would have gladly adopted themselves. Irish engineering expertise was equal to that found elsewhere.

Test Data Analysis (Figure 2)

It should be noted here that all comparitive data is relevant to a cut-off of 25 per cent, irrespective of valve type or number of cylinders. The '305' data, taken directly from indicator charts, has been corrected to 25 per cent from the 33 per cent implied in the diagrams. This 33 per cent is clearly discernible by the sharp discontinuity at point of cut-off, which is a feature of the Marshall gear movement, fully open before sharp closure at the required point.

The chart concocted from the test data available shows the progressive development of the 4-4-0 by Maunsell starting from the baseline locomotive, Robert Coey's class '305'. This particular design, as with the other designs attributable to Coey, was conceived in collaboration with Maunsell, Coey's deputy, so it makes a logical starting point for tracing advances in 4-4-0 performance made by Maunsell. It also is the only Coey 4-4-0 for which indicator diagrams are immediately available.

The first development by Maunsell we shall consider is, apart from the single example of the class '341' on the GS&WR, the excellent rebuild of the Wainwright 'D' and 'E' into

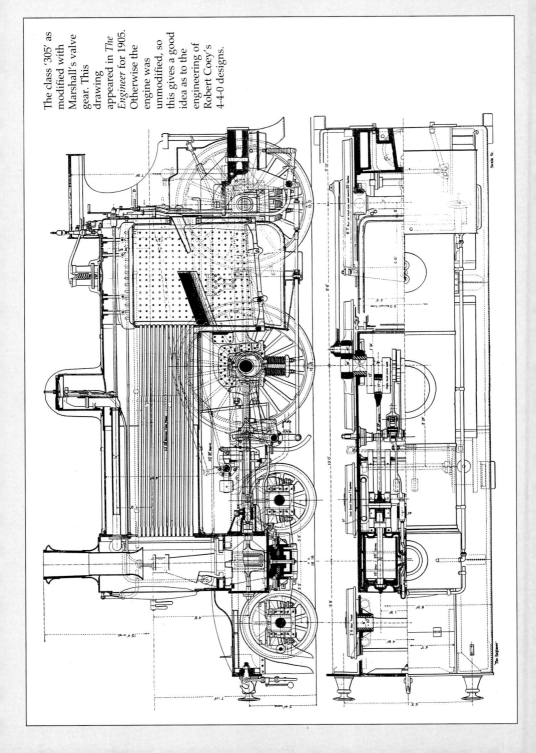

The class '305' as modified with Marshall's valve gear. This drawing appeared in *The Engineer* for 1905. Otherwise the engine was unmodified, so this gives a good idea as to the engineering of Robert Coey's 4-4-0 designs.

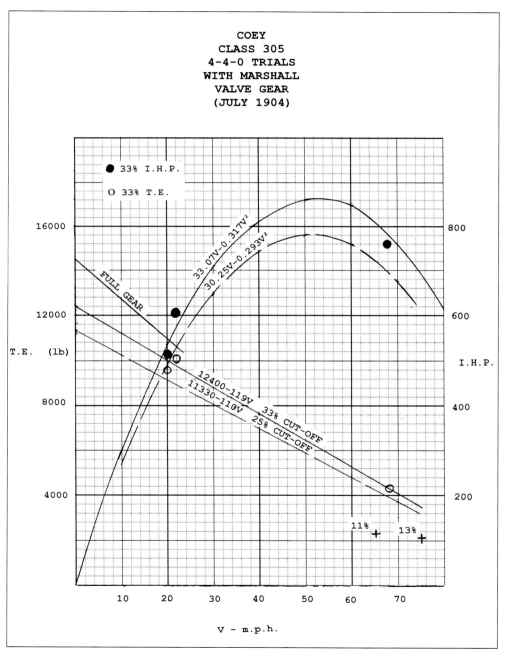

Figure One: Class '305' 4-4-0 trials with Marshall valve gear, July 1904.

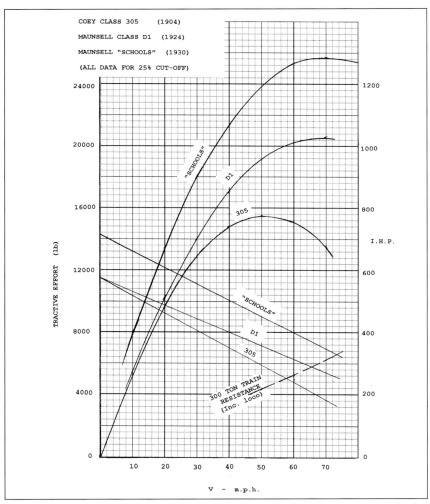

Figure Two: Power chart comparison; class '305', Maunsell class 'D1', Maunsell 'Schools'.

the 'D1' and 'E1'. The 'D1' is being used as the example here as, in its original unmodified form, it was contemporary to the '305' in terms of design date. The major engineering change from the 'D' to 'D1' was the changing of the old-fashioned short-travel slide valves to more efficient long-travel piston valves. The plot shows the clear advantage of long-travel valves on the 'D1', in that the speed for maximum power output is considerably higher than that for the slide valves of the class '305', pointing to a free running locomotive. The higher slope of the TE line for the '305' also indicates throttling of the exhaust caused by short valve events, even allowing for the Marshall gear fitted enhancing exhaust freedom a considerable amount. The steam passages for slide valves are not ideal and some measure of restriction is clearly to be implied.

The 'D1s' were also superheated in the rebuilding, so some degree of the power increase will also come from the greater expansiveness attributed to superheated steam.

Coey never got to the application of superheating on any of his express types, except for some initial experimental work.

When we compare the 'Schools' class with the 'D1', the immediate impression is the even greater maximum power due to two factors, firstly the increased boiler pressure (220 psi as against 180 psi of the 'D1') plus the impact of the 3-cylinder layout. Looking at the slope of the TE line, that of the 'Schools' appears to be steeper than the 'D1'. This is logical, as there is more mechanical friction from the three sets of motion which must increase at a greater rate relative to speed than that for two sets. Analysis of data on the 'N1' and 'N' has indicated the same trend for 3-cylinder over 2-cylinder on that family of designs.

Coal consumption figures as are available are given in *Table A* for typical train weights experienced during the initial service of each locomotive:

Table A

Type	Train weight (Tons)	Coal consumption (lb./ton mile)
Coey class '305'	250	0.140
Maunsell 'D1'	300	0.133
Maunsell 'Schools'	345	0.112

The 'D1' improvement, for a heavier train weight, relative to the '305' is clearly the impact of superheating on coal consumption, plus of course some gain due to the freer running characteristics given by long travel valves. The further improvement attributable to the 'Schools' will be due to technical improvements available to a new generation of locomotive design, i.e. higher boiler pressures, better mechanical efficiency and, of course, the three-cylinder layout giving a smoother transmission of power.

In terms of ihp per ton of locomotive weight the best of these three locomotives appears to be the 'D1' at 19.7 which just beats the 'Schools' value of 19.0. The Coey '305' is commendably high at 16.3 hp/ton for a saturated engine of earlier vintage. However, this is partly due to the weight limitation imposed by the Irish axle load limit then current (1904) of 16 tons over many of the secondary lines which led to lightweight construction techniques. In fact, by 1914, some frames were showing signs of fatigue, necessitating rebuilding with stronger, thicker, material once the axle load limit had been increased, but that is another story.

Summary

What, then, can be said about Maunsell's developments of that archetypal British express locomotive, the 4-4-0? The evidence shows that with correct application of design advances, this compact type, with its inherent stability over reverse curves, low mechanical losses and relatively low production cost proved to be capable of matching many larger six-coupled types in terms of speed and train weight. In the words of Holcroft, the final 4-4-0 offering of Maunsell was 'the best value for money ever put on rails'. It had, however, been arrived at over nearly a quarter of a century of developmental exercises. Its roots lay in those early days at Inchicore, where Maunsell had, under the competent guidance of Robert Coey, gathered his expertise for use in later years.

References:
1. *The Engineer*, 3rd November, 1905.
2. *Locomotive Adventure*, Vol. 2., H. Holcroft.

Bibliography

50 Years of Railway Life by Joseph Tatlow (?)
Derby Works and Midland Locomotives by J.B. Radford (Ian Allan)
Irish Railways in Colour by Tom Ferris (Midland Publishing)
Irish Standard Gauge Railways by Tom Middlemass (David & Charles)
Irish Steam by O.S Nock (Ian Allan)
Locomotive Adventure by H. Holcroft (Ian Allan)
Master Builders of Steam by H.A.V. Bulleid (Ian Allan)
Maunsell Locomotives by Brian Haresnape (Ian Allan)
'Modern Locomotives of the GS&WR' by E.E. Joynt, *The Locomotive* for 1917-18
One Hundred and Fifty Years of Irish Railways by Fergus Mulligan (Appletree Press)
Proceedings of the Institution of Civil Engineers
Munites of the Association of Railway Locomotive Engineers
Proceedings of the Institution of Mechanical Engineers
Railway Gazette, various
Railway Magazine, various
Richard Maunsell, An Engineering Biography by J.E.Chacksfield (Oakwood Press)
'Some Inchicore Proposals' by R.N. Clements, Journal IRRS, Oct. 1973
The Aspinall Era by H.A.V. Bulleid, Ian Allan
The Engineer, 1879
'The Magic of Old Ireland' - Tony Porter, *Railway Magazine* (1991)
The Northern Counties Railway by J.R.L. Currie (David & Charles)
The Works (150 years of Inchicore) by Greg Ryan (CIE)

Index

Numbers in **bold** type refer to illustrations.